# Northwest Passage

Wayne Luckmann

Published by Wayne Luckmann, 2024.

While every precaution has been taken in the preparation of this book, the publisher assumes no responsibility for errors or omissions, or for damages resulting from the use of the information contained herein.

NORTHWEST PASSAGE

**First edition. January 26, 2024.**



ISBN: 979-8224304288

Written by Wayne Luckmann.

# Contents
# The Portable Cage

# WAYNE LUCKMANN

# Northwest Passage

# 47 degrees North

# Poet's Choice

# Sauntering

# Encounters

# Poems on Occasion

# Epiphanies

# Secular Saints

Descartes in Stockholm
    Spinoza at the Hague
    Kant in Konigsberg
    John Stuart Mill at Avignon
    William James in the Adirondacks
    Bertrand Russell On Denoting
    Wittgenstein in Wien
    Camus in Sens
    Oppenheimer at Trinity Test Site
    Bronowski in East Hampton
    Eiseley in the City of Brotherly Love
    Hawking in the Nebula on the Sword of Orion

# Second Series

Matthew Arnold at Liverpool
Sartre in Saint-Germain-des-Prés

# Envoi
# Acknowledgments
# Afterword

# The Portable Cage
## The Prelude

As my soul buds
   then spreads its green
   translucent
   fabric
   toward the sun
   revealing veins
   revealing fibers
   toughened into cellulose
   spirit pooled
   to living matter
   absorbed
   fused and formed
   to structures as delicate
   and strong as bones
   that sometimes bend
   or break
   and mend again,
   if Spirit—
   Soul
   is strong enough
   to heal world wounds
   the ragged holes
   of gnawing worms
   exposing fibers
   to the desiccating wind,
   if heartwood grows,
   how can it hold,
   will spirit spiral toward

glowing autumn rain
or silvered twirling sunlight?
The quality of cellulose
the purity of transformation
the clarity of distillate
will tell

# The Legacy

A concertina
    marbled red
    with ivory button keys
    sang on warm nights
    The world became
    a concertina,
    the night ripe
    with melody
    from rushing air
    A red concertina
    with ivory button keys
    sang hushed sweet sounds
    on summer nights
    while dark cold beer
    foamed in heavy glasses
    and stilled soft voices
    hidden in the warm blue night
    God! How I despised
    that gray-haired man
    who played the concertina
    on warm blue nights
    Each Christmas
    he gave us silver coin
    in exchange
    for bristled cheeks
    Now
    the concertina
    lies in heavy dust
    Once
    we sat on summer porches

watched the traffic moving by
and heard the distant
creaking screen door
slamming
to

# Nuremburg Revisited

Suddenly
    I see those screaming
    men before the multitude
    I see the vast red flags
    With white circles
    and twisted black crosses
    I see torches, high stone walls
    packed hordes heated
    in the hot June night
    Then
    I hear the frenzied cries
    returned
    again,
    again,
    again,
    again
    Until the massive wave of sound
    echoes thunder from the walls
    the minds
    the souls of men
    and echoes
    still
    My grandfather—
    he was there
    from whose loins
    my mother came
    Who in her turn
    whelped me
    in the heavy heat
    of a hot June night

# Kiji Thinking

One warm, starry summer night,
    Beyond bright days upon the lake,
    Beyond green calm of evening water,
    We rode an unknown, winding road
    That seemed so wide my spirit
    Swelled with pungent fields,
    Silted corn, burning skies
    Deepening toward night.
    We came up a carnival.
    The gathering night was ripe
    With colored lights. We walked
    On straw among closed booths
    And came upon a darkened ride.
    My mother said,
    "Remember when we went on this
    The year before we married?
    I got sick, it went so fast."
    I saw a rafter crushed beneath another.
    Evening shadows fell between the beams.
    A sign shut out the bright maze of carnival.
    Then within the heavy silence,
    Darker as we drove away,
    I heard a distant bugle call
    From somewhere
    At the limits of my mind.

# Séance

In memory
    that hawk soars
    still suspended
    there above
    the stirring
    green plush contours
    of undulant moraine
    flowing to the silver drop
    of distant lake
    gouged eons ago

# Adam on the Morning After

A sleepless night upon the hill
   delivered him to a dawn
   that held a color
   he couldn't name.
   Bloodshot, he dropped—
   thick streets, sharp sounds,
   strong smells, houses,
   yellowed stores, anxious people
   pre-occupied along the way thinned.
   Half-alive, deposited,
   he shivered in a tantalizing wind.
   Swaddled on green vinyl,
   cradled, settled, sagged,
   he slumbered, resuming peace,
   pursuing dreams, his former life.
   Around him, figures swam
   like quivering shadows,
   until the door collapsed,
   the coins rebounded, then rejoined—
   And there across the aisle,
   a vision, she appeared,
   soft, quiet,
   gazing out the window
   past his clearing head.
   He squirmed erect.
   he took her in—
   her chestnut hair, her royal
   shimmering blouse, her rich,
   black slacks, drum skin tight,
   the purple flower,

plundered from an early bed,
held within the slender hand
posed upon a yellow, wicker purse.
He stared,
until the mystic beauty of her vacant eyes,
her hovering smile,
turned him in upon himself
and made him doze.
Then she was gone—
Beyond the print-thick pane,
discovering ripe hemispheres of rhythmic flesh,
he saw her move among
the savage crowd
that took her in,
While
the chortling beast fouled the air,
jostled him against the body at his side,
then charged with him
descending to the vast, closed city
bristling on the alluvial plain.

# The Haunting

(For Jack Pearce)
    San Diego Balboa Park
    The Museum of Man
    Somehow still haunt me
    With the bones
    Of a Mayan woman
    Packed in dry earth
    Within a glass case
    And I still stand alone
    Above her gazing
    at an endless darkness
    Of eyeless sockets
    ivory femurs
    Full tooth grin
    Free from flesh
    And I still turn to move
    Toward blinding sunlight
    The dead end
    Of a Sunday afternoon
    And see the perfect hemisphere
    Of bounded sky
    The huddled form
    Upon the blazing grass
    An inert friend too tired
    To share with me
    Until we drop toward Tijuana
    Sit within dry fading heat
    And watch the matador
    Brilliant in a Suit of Lights
    Dominate the beast

And spill the blood
upon the yellow sand
We leave in peace
Lingering among the crowd
To watch ripe women with loose
Full breasts, full hips, heated loins
Smile against the deepening night
That comes to drown us in the stars

# Appearances

Fleeing wasted streets
   Of wandering ghosts
   with dark dead eyes,
   we cross the gleaming
   river lined with ships
   that now make their
   slow way to the ocean,
   past docks bristling
   with cranes heaving
   huge cargo of luxuries
   from foreign ports
   Crossing the bridge
   that spans what once
   was verdant valley
   now cross-hatched
   with glistening railroad
   tracks crowded with
   boxcars, boxcars, boxcars
   where indigent people once met
   in reconciliation and renewal,
   high on a green hill against
   the glistening skyline
   of girded storage tanks,
   majestic image of grand hotel,
   tall church spire, the silhouette
   of pioneer log cabin
   whose roof I often climbed,
   sitting on the peak to gaze
   in rapture at the world
   until I eased to the edge,

dropped to cinders and the hill's rim
from whose top I often tumbled
rolling until sky and clouds spun,
I scrambling up reached the lagoon
with redbrick arches of boat house
long gone replaced by poured concrete
beside lime green water
where ghosts of small boys
file along mud-slick banks
waiting for the tug of phantom fish

# Adam on the Morning After

A sleepless night upon the hill
    delivered him to a dawn
    that held a color he couldn't name
    Bloodshot he dropped through
    teeming streets, sharp sounds,
    strong odors of anxious people
    pre-occupied along the way
    Half-alive, he shivered
    in a tantalizing wind,
    deposited on green vinyl,
    he settled swaddled,
    sagged to slumber
    resuming peace pursuing
    fleeing dreams of a former life
    Around him figures
    swam like quivering shadows
    until the door collapsed,
    coins rebounded then rejoined
    and there across the aisle
    she appeared, soft, quiet,
    gazing out the window
    past his clearing head
    He squirmed erect
    to take her in:
    her chestnut hair,
    her royal purple
    shimmering blouse,
    her rich black slacks
    drum skin tight,
    a purple flower

plundered
from an early bed
she held within
her slender hand
upon a yellow, wicker purse
He stared transfixed
until the mystic beauty
of her vacant eyes
her fixed smile
turned him in
upon himself
and made him
doze
Then she was gone:
Beyond the pane
of print-smeared glass
discovering ripe hemispheres
of rhythmic flesh he saw her
move among the savage crowd
that took her in
While the chortling beast fouled
the air jostling him against the body
at his side then charged on with him
descending to the vast closed city
bristling on the alluvial plain

# Seminar Satori

He flounders in a feeble light half dead
    A voice drones on at the limits
    of a glistening varnished tabletop
    He seeks beyond the gleaming
    window frame and sees
    the stick thin tree
    A lone red leaf turns in the wind
    twirling on the black wet branch
    when suddenly it stops
    translucent in a radiant glow
    He stares transfixed until the sudden
    exultation of a bird with one sharp note
    cuts him from the glistening branch
    back to stale aspirations
    in the closed, dim room
    When he looks again
    a naked tree
    bends against
    the bitter wind

# Windfall
## (For Vincent)

The year's descent
   brings rain
   mist steeps streets
   redeeming them
   brooding clouds
   subdue gray concrete
   trappings I leave behind
   Soft sudden wind tugs
   leaves from glistening trees
   scattering them
   cementing them to pavement
   like old wet newsprint
   And suddenly
   The world is leaves
   wet yellow leaves
   brown leaves
   green leaves
   quivering leaves
   tinged with red
   Until
   the wind dies
   and I descend

# Vacation Stop

The bridge again he calmly
   starts across passing people
   on the hallowed wood beneath his feet.
   Students wondrously intent in distant rooms
   glance his way but hardly notice that he's here
   Autumn leaves cast upon the bank,
   spilling water rushing over rocks
   flowing toward the Bay,
   all these recall the quiet night
   his Lady talked about the sound
   water makes flowing over rocks
   "I like the way it falls," she said,
   as it fell clean, clear, flowing
   from the Berkeley hills
   The night was mild
   A light wind troubled twigs on trees
   Overhead, the distant stars
   bright against the dark curved sphere
   fled from them where they stood
   together on the bridge she against
   the wooden rail he behind her pressing in
   until the fog closed down and drove them
   through the glow of mystic streets
   searching for the pungent warmth of muted
   yellow lights, billowing smoke, babbling
   voices where at a marble table,
   he stroked her with his words,
   but later in the plush of her rich abode
   they grappled in hushed restraint
   that urged him on to grope

soft flesh that never yielded

# To Louis Simpson on Seeing a Poem and Explanation in The American Scholar

I've asked myself as you advised
    if all of this is really needed.
    But once again your poem surprised me.
    Perhaps the shock of seeing you again
    having seen you live though distant
    heard you talk on Blake and Wordsworth
    in the class I had from you at Berkeley
    the year they killed a president
    How could you know me sitting there in back
    wondering about the details of your life?
    For I had heard you read your poems
    within a hot closed room in Kroeber Hall
    Do you remember as we left
    the stirring night, the mild spring wind
    the sharp, vibrant, piercing female cry
    from darkened streets beneath black pregnant
    hills seeded with the yellow points of light?
    But all of this seems quite beside the point.
    Let it pass. What really interests me, however,
    what really made me want to write
    was what I felt on seeing
    "Indian Country" with your note
    about that image of a man in Minnesota.
    You said how difficult that image
    was in being born and exorcised.
    Well, might I say the same about myself?
    Remember how the poisoned air

gave the towering grove of peeling
eucalyptus a ghostly look beneath
a hazy, smog-bound California sky?
I searched the streets, the blurring flash
of streaming cars and suddenly you passed,
met my eyes as I met yours.
How I hoped for recognition
while the shock of seeing you
made me follow as you disappeared.
Now having read again your poem and note
I somehow feel compelled to ask:
Did I see disappointment in your face?
Did you see mine from empty promises,
insistent hollow words that still sustained
the pulse of overwhelming ache
to flee, to love, abandoning the world
in reckless wild exhilarating consummation
of a mad desire fading through dissipation
foreshadowing the end I knew must come
even as I walked, saw you pass, glance at me,
then rush away leaving me troubled,
so unsatisfied moving toward the wooden bridge
I stood upon alone above the quiet stream
beneath green veins of sunlight
through translucent leaves,
hearing flowing water falling
over slowly wearing rock.
Forgive me.
I'm sorry now I've spent your time.
For now I know that man you saw,
that ghostly figure dark against
the burnished, autumn sky must be a sign:

Walt Whitman waiting somewhere
by the roadside alone and puzzled
leaning on a stubborn bumper jack
wondering how that ratcheting beside
a freeway had anything at all to do
with twilight stars above an endless prairie.

# An Unmailed Letter

## I

Seeing you recalled the love.
    Sudden loss quelled by time,
    reduced to dulled residual,
    renewed once more on seeing
    you again.
    How utterly surprised I was,
    hearing of you as I did,
    that you were there just as before,
    existing in that very place as I.
    When I reached back, time overwhelmed
    me, pinned me to the hard, enduring
    wall of moments past all hope,
    past all reliving.
    The phone call, I admit,
    was quite impulsive.
    Why had I called?
    I sometimes wonder even now.
    Memory, perhaps, or hope, perhaps,
    compelled my expectation of your interest
    conveyed to me by accident and I had found you.
    I sat upon a transient bed,
    my naked feet upon the plush, rich rug,
    listening to the droning air-conditioner,
    the vast night beyond the walls
    and ceiling of the room in which I sat,
    the troubled glow from distant cities
    with lights as myriad as muted stars
    above me in the desert night.

How your voice stunned me
when I on impulse called
and you had answered.

# II

Seeing you again I looked for change.
    Most everything seemed the same.
    Lost years were unimportant,
    dismissed as hardly ever having been.
    Yet, how I wished those intervening
    years could be vanquished and restored
    by the vibrancy and the keenness
    of the moment I was there, you were there.
    We truly still existed, our love
    (I call it love)
    had held despite the crush of days
    and mitigating years.
    Then all those things hardly noticed
    came back at me and snatched me up in time:
    Your sons whom I had never seen
    greeting me with questioning eyes
    that made me think of distant mountains.
    The shaggy beast, more bear than dog,
    that as a pup had run with me along the beach
    through hissing foam, on wet, packed sand.
    How she had leapt, bounding floppy-eared
    and big-pawed leaving dark prints that scored
    then mingled with my own straight serious trail
    I left behind me as I gazed upon dark ocean
    where it met the dazzling sky,
    I searching for a sign, an answer to the question
    only answered now sitting in your home
    sapped by heat, conscious of the droning fan,
    the dog grown gross and idle from stifling heat
    and mitigating years.

Still, you both seemed much the same:
He wore no shirt, and in his naked flesh
I saw no softening, no sign of grossness.
He even spoke the same in alternating
moods, first with quiet emphasis bringing
vividness and drama to his words,
then with high elation so that I lived
with you those years again,
and she, too, with shy reserve
save for one wild fling that thrilled
and stunned me with her cry and rush
into my awkward arms.
Yet, in the reporting of our years apart,
I knew the distance we had come alone
For sitting there within the heat
among the trappings and incidental
brick-brack of your lives,
I recalled my first dim-witted thoughts
on reawakening alone,
the daily choice of dreary clothes,
the tedious drive to work
past green, towering hemlock,
weeping birch, red vine-maple,
frail eternal pine,
boundless sky with billowing clouds,
all dulled by my involvement
with worldly things endlessly persisting
in their grind of blurring road
now and then compelling me to think
of you and wonder where you were:
Your farm: what had it looked like?
Your home in Michigan I had never seen

and never would.
All these thoughts were soon repressed.
For when we rose and sat again for lunch,
the talk continued broken by a phone call,
persistent queries from your sons,
my small children, and a pointed glance
that told me then excuses must be made:
Our time was brief, more people should be seen.
You, too, had plans. Your daily lives continued.
ours had merely been suspended.
But when we left, you offered us your home
and teased me with a promise of returning
from your weekend early.

# III

When we returned, dropping from the freeway
   and left behind the rush of lights along the way,
   we found again the flat dark street
   thick with eucalyptus hushed beneath
   the glow of streetlamp and hazy night.
   We found your house, entered with our bags,
   snapped on the fan, undressed the kids
   who woke and crabbed and settled back
   then tried to settle down ourselves.
   My dozing spouse gave up defeated,
   crept to your bed leaving me in a peace
   troubled by a brooding presence that hovered
   in the stillness with the quiet drone of whirling fan.
   So while she and the children muttered
   in the heavy heated darkness of their sleep,
   I wandered through soft light of your hushed house
   and understood how much a home
   it was—as all your houses were—more home
   than house—trying to define what made them
   so much you, such thoughts I had with you not there.
   I saw the substance of your lives:
   I saw the stack of magazines on flying
   in your study along with books that I had read
   and thrilled to discovering beauty and spirit in our lives.
   How I would have loved to share with you that joy,
   much like the joy we shared in reading *Night Flight*.
   All I observed I held as constants.
   Yet, something troubled me: The quiet light?
   Your lingering presence? The mystic, soft vibrations
   of the autoharp I accidentally played my hand across

to hear the whisper of an unintended melody increase
the hush and hallowed stillness of your home.

# IV

I never found the answer there.
    The following dawn, once we had packed,
    while she coaxed the children to dress
    and scrub to their usual, still unusual early
    morning sheen, I searched again, creeping
    through your home, examining one last time
    restoring links to days that bound me to you,
    chain me still.
    I felt unsettled
    The day before miscarried, unfulfilled.
    I asked myself again: How could those years
    be rescued and redeemed? But then, why should they?
    While I prowled one final time, these solitary thoughts
    accompanying me, until I found the yellow card
    and sat and wrote the quick, cryptic note
    that never could, I'm sure, convey my turmoil
    and remorse with you not there.
    All those lost years remained.
    What else remained?
    The quiet of your home compelled me.
    The uncommon quiet of the kids compelled me,
    my whole life and those ten years compelled me
    to snap the final suitcase latch and move.
    The gray walk remained, the stifling
    early morning heat, the unrelenting smog
    already gathering, the naked eucalyptus,
    our car I packed with cases, children, alienated
    spouse, all these made clear the moment
    I made a final study of your house,
    then dipped into a cycle of routine that whirled

me once again toward distant mountains,
toward desert roads and bitter loss
that lay beyond.

# The Prairie

These rolling hills worn
    through to rock
    and everywhere hosannas
    from bright fields of sunflowers
    along the perfect road
    we travel on for days
    toward home
    past weathered dwellings
    slate-gray
    ghostly sentinels
    that seem abandoned
    even though
    the signs show habitation:
    Ballooning wash
    upon the line
    waves to us
    lonely as a woman
    lost to the prairie wind
    raising frantic arms
    against the billowing clouds
    that reach from mountains

# Closed Circuit

The world, the quarrel,
    my dying rage behind me
    I descend through thick bushes
    to a darkened street
    Winter wind sways branches
    Of a weeping birch soughing out
    black leaves against bleak winter sky,
    sharp wind among the branches
    of a pine seems almost like a sigh
    toward gray clouds strung out
    in fallow ridges above a stick-thin
    tree bending in the bitter wind
    A dark and listing house:
    And though I know that houses
    do not feel, this sagging house
    in winter light seems sad:
    The upper window shades are eyes
    those shades just shades half-drawn
    obscuring hollow darkened rooms
    recall the frail old woman
    in hanging clothes
    who left this empty house
    The monkey tree sways
    from perfection rigid at the top
    destroyed until the spines swoop down
    curve back in dark parabola
    toward clouds and barren sky above
    my old ungrowling car beside the concrete
    walk that leads me to a tarnished key
    among the join of other keys upon the ring,

the key within the glimmering lock unlatching,
and then the yellow warmth and urgent,
piercing cry of children home.

# Epithalamium

What difference should it make
   That their two bodies met
   That rigid flesh in yielding flesh
   Made loins respond wet with joy
   Glad for union when she rose
   To join with him and guide him in
   I'm not that changed.
   My legs still move
   My feet still feel
   the troubled earth,
   The trembling earth
   still spins around a dying sun,
   The self-consuming sun
   still seeks a distant star
   The cold, dwarfed stars
   flee outward from us
   Toward utter darkness
   What difference should it make
   That I had let her be my sun
   That I had dwelled within her light,
   That I had whirled eccentric circles
   Bound to dreams of distant stars
   Now my sun should be the moon
   And I the earth in sinuous
   Path around her would join
   Her to me
   Then while moving
   In conjunction
   Bound in union
   Though we moved apart

Separate yet not in isolation
Cold muted stars
Would flee from us
And leave us to our universe

# Nonce on a Theme by Sandburg

What if I had never met you, Joan
    or the kids had never come?
    That day I spoke to you in class
    to ask about your notes,
    what if I had turned away?
    Instead I invited you to coffee
    hauled along my fears
    to where among a host
    of Nobel laureate scientists
    I quarreled with you.
    The Berkeley hills warming
    in the sun, tall cascading pines
    on slopes, bright morning mist
    joined the clash of voices, loud
    clamoring coffee cups until
    I watched the slow sinuous rhythm
    of your hips that stung with such
    desire it never healed
    and lust lingering quelled
    suspended in a Daly City night

# Running the Maze

I rise still troubled
   from my dream
   then pound through
   vacant morning streets
   swept with debris
   beneath the throbbing
   caution light past vacant
   stores with empty shelves,
   assertive signs directing me
   Dark figures stir
   at corner bus stops
   Dark shapes define
   the labyrinth of the street
   beneath the trembling clouds
   that trap the gathering light
   becoming dawn

# A Communion of Saints

(Ode to Walt Whitman)
    Single spiders
    in a thousand webs
    hold the dawn,
    snag the feeble sun
    melting morning fog
    dew on leaves
    dispersing them,
    objects of the world
    revealed again
    restored
    Green girders
    of a spanning bridge
    whose brick and mortar
    battlements support the vigilance
    A lone watchman spends
    a solitary life impaled
    reads in a tower as I pass by
    toward personal disasters
    spun from singular affairs

# Reconnaissance

"The best time of our lives,"
    one said at the year's dead end.
    Another offered a toast
    we all accepted
    rising from our chairs
    to stand on them
    spontaneity brimmed
    to thoughtless laughter.
    So begun,
    hope for the burgeoning year
    ripened to disasters:
    Our fractured lives
    wept rich discoveries
    beyond our bargaining:
    A long day's journey
    from that brief spell
    we met, touched spirits,
    fled the contact,
    we all were lost
    solitary wanderers
    through the desert
    of our own dark night.

# Accident/Incident

That day of thin, cool autumn light
    on livid trees felled to rise again
    in pre-cast concrete buildings,
    why did you reach for me?
    We touched in perfect stillness
    and heard the buzz and busy hum
    of silence from hidden wires in empty
    offices with carpeting of lush corridors
    hung miraculously among trees in dwellings
    planned to keep us from the ripened earth

# Forced March

(Five Poems with Commentary)

I

Some thistles are like people:
Once you step descending
through the grass and ditch
you see the world all thorns
inviting, testing, teasing,
inviting touch while holding
out a warning: such adaptations
of the flesh that snag
the toughest calloused skin
keep you off yet flower
in soft summer rain

II

Soft blossoms fill the purple air
ripe with beauty while mist yellows
headlights of distant cars
along the guarded freeway,
tortured beasts laboring through
the rise to soar then coast again
descending through a thick wash
of tires and sweet poisoning
of rich exhaust that reach us
where we watch bound
by multitudes of angry thistle
under dripping skies

III

Why should I be so interested in thistle?
Why interested in an eighteen-wheel
snub-nosed brute that baffles

to the rise then coasts descending
beneath dark dripping skies?
Why you were there remembering
whom you lived with (call it marriage)
who gave you coin in children
never minted stamped with love
that I denied examining
his indelible design
while I watched that truck
through a hedge of angry thistle
IV
The spray of light proclaimed
its coming with sound that often
bolted us from dreams
by loudly heralding
through rippled shacks
I reached for you
urged you through the cut
where we dropped and waited
beneath old timbers of the bridge
while the sudden silent ponderous
form surprised us, its mass, weight,
heavy rumbling purpose,
a sword of light flamed out
before it as it swept across,
boxcars followed singing
on their wheels swaying
in the rhythm of their rush
of stirring air
The silence from the last
car following as we climbed,
turned toward the track

glistening from dark rain again
as you spun off almost in pursuit
hair frantic in the glow
of warning light
permitting passage
I followed
bent to lift the flesh and bones
your head bent to indicate
then paced the sleepers
my rough hands beneath
the belly still filled with life
When we arrived
you hurried for the spade
We paused quietly agreed
the front lot by the walk
close by the track
between jagged stumps
of maple trees that once
had worried someone
I manned the tool,
stood on the blade
shearing through
the rain-wet matting
of the grass to reach
brown soil, dry solid earth
that shaped into a box I dug,
took the heap arranging
it for ripening, gently piled
the earth, replaced the ragged
sod, and stepped on it
pressing it to dark repose
V

The following night
we climbed a tree
opening like a ripened
vault beneath a nave
of leaves in green ghostly light
where we clung to buttressing
limbs offering foundation
for new growth from ribs
that twined and thinned
flattening into leaves
revealing veins
(Commentary)
Small insects
belly up and die
along the margins
of my yellow page
I thrash
to excavate
my lost
discoveries


Civilization and Its Dissonance
    All things give rise to poetry:
    A vision of the world
    from a high tower:
    Black wet streets below
    glistening with jewels,
    gutters running with gems
    of sunlight and debris
    A frail old man
    with burnished wood cane,

black frayed coat
all time and essence
following his long shadow
down the hill to the bright
bristling street
The small dark figure
of a woman at the vast
glass pane high above
the snarled, concrete freeway
below, her arms resigned
across her breasts
while watching traffic
The cross-hatched flow
of rain on the windshield
of a parked car
The soaked Madrona trees
their blood-red peeling skins
their green leaves swaying
in the wind-whipped rain \
throughout a long, dark day

# Leave Taking

## I

She drove off
  searching for a spot
  to light some foreign place
  where she could write,
  learn to love herself
  safe from all previous contact
  Her car seemed toy-like
  Yet in it she had braved the desert
  dropped in, exchanged disasters
  hers for mine , slipped
  faults in our former lives:
  She too had reached to touch
  was left alone abandoned
  She disappeared,
  the sound of her
  small red car
  diminishing
  taking leave

**II**

In the garden
    along the public paths
    that coil upon me
    something nicks my heel
    I spin
    to challenge it
    A moving point,
    the flightless bee
    walks home
    leaves the asphalt
    starting out on busy
    unadapted legs
    across the wasteland
    of sun-bled pebbles
    sticks, stones, debris,
    dead droppings
    from desert plants,
    a place rife with lizards
    monstrous in proportion
    basking on baked rocks
    remnants of nearby mountains
    by some ancient
    accident surging
    from the desert floor
    above my head

# III

Bees in the flowering shrubs
    outside my private door
    work all day and live to work
    returning from the garden
    of the world
    to the dark droning hive
    giving up their load
    both mind and social store
    to the swarm of purpose
    home safe from all living things
    man, beast, or serpent

# The Poet Considers Zhivago

No wolves
    howl
    outside my door
    In the dawn
    reluctant motors
    whine
    then rise above
    the pounding
    of a man
    beginning work
    breaking free
    yesterday's cement
    and last night's
    dream

# Fourth Floor North

(For Anna Marie)
    The morning wake:
    the city to the west
    heaves to its wreath
    of hills with garnishing
    of trees and scattered sprigs
    of dwellings in the dull
    sluggish dawn
    Then tinker-legged, leggo-toyed
    the slabs of city towers
    burnished by the sun
    the windows to the east
    open to the brutal eminence
    of mountains: dark purple hulks
    probe the bright bands of sky
    one salmon-fleshed
    another as blue as glacial ice
    seeping to the river of our days
    the burdened cones of hemlock
    the sinless dome of my
    estranged daughter's school
    That heaved hollow bears
    the load hunching towards
    heaven and the endless
    silence that renews an agony
    of longing and brings
    a haunting presence:
    the silver sectioned sphere
    I gaped at as a child
    raised as I was on

forbidden rooftops pulling
myself across the rain trough
my gorged heart throbbing
on the asphalt plain
rich with gems of
summer sunlight until
I stand straddling the peak
and gaze in wonder
at the bright basilica
grand in its glory
hovering in the distant
shimmering air
This labored room
the wasted heap beneath
soiled shroud of sheets
who bore our sorrow glows
crimson in the imminence
of dawn. This strangled
room gagged with stale
afterbirth and bitter aftertaste
of night and grief contaminating
the watch we keep
to celebrate her passage
From such brief gifts
of moments we bear
the burden of our years
our joys and rosary
of sorrows our legacy
of death, the rhythm
and the slow extrusion
of our days

# Barn Cleaning

The droppings of the man
    whose house I live in
    make me conscious of my own,
    so edging dissolution
    I sweep aside his spore,
    the one I've seen all over town.
    Here again are his remains:
    leaves transformed from trees
    sent as letters seeking gain
    from get–rich-quick schemes;
    navigation charts preserved
    religiously as scrolls;
    stored fishing gear:
    hooks, gaffs, battered hats
    intimations of some brief joy;
    rubble of pre-cut lumber,
    unhung cobbled cabinets;
    toys of children grown and fled;
    deposits of a wife left wretched
    wrenched from her marriage shell
    screaming down a curse
    on both the living and the dead
    dropping me to stillness and debris.
    The shock brings pause:
    Here at the lip of my fortieth year
    I wonder at the road ahead
    although I know where it leads.
    Suddenly, barn cleaning
    seems like bridge burning.

# Marathon

He sets out on his self-appointed rounds
    The light mere intimation of the dawn
    dilutes the darkness. Still houses
    blind windows frame the night
    The world in its ponderous track
    curves through its seasons
    peopled by sleeping dogs he lets lie
    made manifest by ditch debris
    the stuff of life:
    unwrapped wrappings
    bottles empty of spirit unreclaimed
    plastic casings; synthetic cloth;
    stillborn leavings: a cocoon of artificial
    foreskin as quickly spent and shed
    as last night's love
    He makes the extra mile
    pounds by the continental transport
    revved to life rumbling at idle
    its massive metal rattling charged
    with purpose and power
    Above him in the sphere
    of its infinite dark determined course
    Orion, the hunter, races on always ahead

# The Whale

For all our waking moments
    we say more
    in our sleep:
    So she in the clear blue beauty
    of her dream sounds
    the depths of loneliness
    Sweet wind puckers
    from her lips
    both here and behind
    two soft openings
    of our complicated worm
    sing of the whale
    who sounding
    sucks in life
    fish, fowl (feathers and all)
    belching cries
    that seem like song
    the flesh she wears
    protects her
    from the rime-chilled
    bitter winter sea
    while my flesh melts
    I feel the cold gray wind
    beneath the rattling door

# The Sacrament

Our separate days gather through the seasons,
    a chronicles of disasters, frequent dissolutions,
    anniversaries of our birth, our lives brief and uncertain,
    As delicate as flowers each year dormant under
    furrowed clouds, winter rain until spring when
    bare trees bristle fanning stick-thin branches
    toward the sun swell to multitudes of purple buds
    So my life gathered in that moment as radiant
    as a globe beading on a ripening vine one bright
    day gathering through its seasons bringing wonder
    and quiet joy of new beginning from one cautious
    searching, doubtful touch
    Nurtured by a warm brilliance of flowering
    fragrance, the crushed foil of open water
    winnowing in a mild breeze beneath blue bird
    sky and mellow sun, my life gathered through
    its seasons swelling out of darkness into love

# **Singularity**

Out of your whole life
    that one brief spell
    of kindness when a gentle
    boy placed himself behind
    you , braced himself and
    pushed the schoolyard
    swing to send your thin
    body towards the heaving
    tumult of towering autumn
    clouds
    You swung
    that one sweet time
    until your singular desire
    fulfilled left you breathless
    Your heart would burst
    Three decades
    a hundred dreams
    a thousand defeats later
    you long for gorgeous
    men to save you from
    the sucking sink of years:
    dark shadows now crowd
    your gem-clear eyes,
    age blemishings disguised
    by subtle daily masks
    of skilled deceptions,
    the wonder and the peril
    of chemistry.
    My dream dies just as hard:
    I am no gorgeous man.

I offered you a full account
the steady consummation
of my love so unaware
of what I wished for
giving you my life,
my work, my soul
for one brief spell
and paid the price
for your consistency
singular and firm.

# Degrees of Separation

The orange cat that wandered
    into my yard to stay and daily feed
    then peed on me while I held it
    old, sick, feeble going to the vet
    recalls the orange cat in Berkeley
    whose angry remains I found
    the day we moved conjuring
    the yellow tom that slept
    with the little black and tan dog
    that one day was gone
    I contended too frequently
    with that orange cat in Berkeley,
    why, I have never understood,
    but it got even by first vanishing
    much to the sorrow of two small children
    only revealing its skull as I pulled away
    the flattened boxes from the corner of a shed,
    my shock only partly due to my just
    having said farewell to a woman, nineteen,
    with whom I was involved platonically
    (despite my having wanted more)
    and I just had traded barbs with my spouse
    after said young woman and I had lunched
    to bid adieu. Then I found the cat and while
    I listened to the *Concierto de Aranjuez*
    swell through summer screens settling among
    the flowering bougainvillea, all my longing
    gushed from me into sparkling sunlight
    Later in our new setting my spouse got even
    by having yet another affair

And the virginal young woman?
She sent a pleasant note announcing
her engagement with someone
she had dated without my knowing
all the while I royally courted her.

# Leaving the Yellow House

Everything about this place reveals a man
  who loved to do things with his hands:
  Bird feeders line the garden fence posts;
  outside the kitchen picture window
  a platform for offering grain. Yet,
  for all these holy stations spilling seed
  there are few birds. A chick-a-dee scolds
  "dee-dee-dee from a drooping sunflower
  blossoming black with decay; the garden
  gone to ruin, black plums shrivel ripe
  oozing yellow on trees; snap beans thick
  and long beyond eating; striped pale green
  squash balloon to All Saints Night
  proportions well before season.
  In the garage below, a shop
  with an old tractor battleship gray
  clean as a vessel on the verge of firing
  into life with one twist of the key.
  Tools scatter on benches dark with oil
  and dirt ready for use on some suspended
  task. Cobwebs decorate the heavy beams
  holding up the rooms above for living.
  In the rooms above, breasts that once
  gorged young men to throb with lust
  now sag in insufficient halters:
  A chorus as ancient as Greece gropes
  and claws through stuff of lives
  gray from the settled dust of years,
  hauling bag after plastic bag crammed
  to bulging sheen with debris someone

had thought too dear to throw away
now dumped sans ceremony in landfill
burial.
Those haggard women bargaining
for claiming rights retrieve from stale
odors of moribund lives objects of little
worth but of great value they will clutch
all the way home to houses teeming
with hordes of gathered items stored
as buried treasure
A strange silence sifts with soft late
summer rain: A poem will surely come
from this proper recompense for my pain,
this sordid effort of my strong back, weak will

# Northwest Passage

Northwest Passage
    (Ode to Walt Whitman)
    Witnessing such things
    before: a book discarded
    fouled as trash buried
    with yellow leaves lost
    among weeds, some ripped
    pages crushed to ragged
    spheres used to entertain
    someone with games:
    why should it touch me?
    Rain for days, bare bushes,
    branches, leafless sticks of trees
    dripped radiant globes when
    unexpected sun, black clouds
    churning into gray let streams
    of winter light break
    through with sudden rays
    from glowing clouds bath the air,
    glistening asphalt, burnishing
    leaves that furled fluttering
    in wet winter wind.
    I swerved to miss what swept
    behind, and as I straightened
    from the curve, an image
    of a man went with me
    compelling me to wonder
    who had tossed that soul
    disdained in misty wind
    that flapped its pages

splattered by the grime
from blasts of swerving cars
The bright sun remained
dazzling from the chariot
ahead where I saw the youth,
his head held so,
one shoulder toward
the wheel, he sat with such
assurance I knew that suit
of brilliant steel repelling
rain drops held for him
his final goal.
I wondered then—
What was I?
An open book.
A wet black winter road.

# Moon Cycle

ER odors
    stinging sweet and sour
    linoleum tile floor
    glaring lights
    wide gleaming doors
    swing closed behind me
    as the gurney
    wheels me in
    My father stands beside me
    offering his hand I cling to
    while I lie on the cold table
    as ghostly attendants robed
    in white straighten and reset
    shattered bone then sew
    my severed tissues not using
    any numbing drug and I grip
    my father's hand so hard
    he cries out in pain
    and I leave bruises,
    he growing angry later
    anytime he should recall
    that distant summer afternoon
    for he nor I can fathom why
    not given any reason why
    I yell and scream and holler
    with all the strength
    of my five years
    crushing his hand trying
    to pass to him my pain
    Three decades later

similar events achieve
a resolution: Now I
the father attend my son
seeking aid for his
severed lip and fractured
teeth the night Apollo Eleven
lands and Neil Armstrong
steps down into lunar dust
While my son suffers
his pain in silence
waiting for the numbing
drug to take effect
before his wound is sutured
the intern and I
in some strange unspoken
collusion take turns sneaking
off to an adjacent room
where we snatch glimpses
of shadowy snowy images
sent back to us from space
through the black void of heaven

# Epithalamion

Among
      the regulated flow
      subdued by traffic stripes
      invincible commands
      of automatic lights
      I flash by
      slow
      stop
      glance behind
      There
      upon the porch
      beneath arches
      thick with hanging
      summer vines
      the bright day
      seems fulfilled
      Yet
      as they stand—
      she radiant, traditional—
      her virginal dress
      the legacy of veil
      he seems
      in his occasional suit
      uneasy
      dark
      He stands aside beside her,
      she posing smiles.
      Perhaps it's just the older
      hovering presence at her back;
      perhaps it's just her sudden

glance at passing traffic
where in the waiting line
I should have called a warning:
"Beware of her!
She too discovering you
will find her fear deposed
her power
her secret joy
will rule!
Watch out for others passing!"
Too late I pass.
Already they descend
beneath the rain of clattering rice

# Tanscoaxial

Light through latticing
    fills this cell with incense
    of warm wood and shadows
    from western sunlight softening
    on hemlock with fir boughs swaying
    in the rush of warm wind
    bringing clear sky a pierian blue
    raising images:
    marianne moore in Brooklyn
    age-lined innocent
    veiled by a curtain
    of bright gossamer filigree
    writing out her spartan prophecies
    at a dark barren desk
    cadences as spare as Aeschylus
    a vision of life from sunlight
    off that bridge neither harp
    nor spire a multitude
    of vectoring wire
    that web still singing praises
    raising song

# Ghetto Room

Too trite for poetry
the rain that flings
and spatters under eaves
the spray and hiss of passing cars
squelched from usual thundering
The squash and creak of footsteps
overhead: All these escape me:
Too personal

# The Dragon Effect at Hurricane Ridge

The wind is hushed that day
    a soft breeze tinged by snow
    stirs from distant peaks lingering
    in winter tingling the late spring
    air chilling the new mild sun
    harbinger of another burgeoning
    year
    From the high promontory
    witnessing a pale sun ripening
    into lavender and orange
    on distant spires and diminished
    towers across the broad swirling
    plain of blue global waters,
    in the silence of hushed stir
    of branch and breeze, he hears
    in his heart's core the clash
    and mesh of commerce,
    the bartered void of shrouded
    residential streets with mute
    facades of rich dwellings.
    He stands transfixed, purged
    finally of bitterness, loneliness,
    and rage sharing again oblivious
    to the portent free from lingering
    gall that will surge again to gorge
    him from another blind alley
    that seems a lifetime but lies
    only seven swift years away.
    But now he willingly climbs
    with her following the vein

of knuckling vertebrae of rock
that runs along the ridge beneath
the lucid sky where he splays,
his flesh, belly, loins pressed
upon the crumbling mountain,
its scaling earth furred with
clinging growth glistening and
crystalline fragments peopled
by tiny beasts exploring
the range and ridges of his
hand and. spread fingers
as if he were one long extrusion
of the wilderness they journey
through
What difference did such
wanderings make ladybird bug,
you in your tidy marvelously
perfect carapace with wings
settling neatly into the red
brilliant black spotted wonder
of your shell?
The ridge a slumbering ancient
dragon sign of good fortune
and good luck rising from crusted
earth on which he rides while
he like a slugged beast lies along
the spine that writhes ascending
the ridge on either side
sluicing to the spare sunlight
glowing on the palisade
of naked pine bone-white
leached sapless pillars bristling

on the steep mountain slope
Riding the dragon's back
he spins with the slow certain
movement of the earth
as small children once rode him
the quiet translucent insect resting
on the promontory of his hand
riding the summit of his knuckle
bones those peaks like distant
pinnacles named for ancient titans
She could laugh then
joined in that joyful union
of dragon insect he
the two of them
one a mote one a mite
upon the vast sheared derma
of an infinitely bounded globe

# Union Bay Village

The early morning sun
    on days like these:
    bright, delicate, warm,
    rich with haze,
    soft with diffusing life
    advent of spring or autumn's
    quivering consummation mustering
    memories a n d ghosts that
    celebrate the raising of these
    regulation houses: the rasp,
    the hammer, the driven nail
    remind us of too frequent
    wars once so great
    they reached beyond our
    wildest expectations and left
    their residue of surplus
    dwellings once sheltering those
    returned as victors seeking
    reparation for their bleeding
    hope, fractured lives, ragged
    souls as fragmented as shattered bone.
    Now third-world tongues
    suddenly transposed transformed
    discourse cadence s that seem
    like song: warblings of transnational
    happenings in scolding cries
    as raucous as early morning crows
    the bickering among tribes
    of children marshaling at bus stops,
    their quarrels learned from conflicts

once offered as a daily portion
of their own native land
While through plywood walls
as thin as barracks boisterous
singing of a Nigerian woman
sweeping out debris, her robe
and headpiece and surging
sound as brilliant as early
morning sunlight ripening
our evanescent dreams


**Beginnings** (Prose Poem)

One found item plucked from a path through trees, a stone I claw from moist, soft earth, this hard teardrop fits firmly in my hand with flat, pointed shape that men who hunted this forest millennia ago might have used to fix a spear for piercing quivering silvery scaled sides of spawning salmon.

I stand alone on this dirt path of soft earth clutching this hard fusion studying the towering trees that soar toward gray overcast, the green spines of ferns and sproutings of fractured rock along the muddy path, the sinuous, fern-choked wash that drops from the high bluff on which I stand and view the gleaming serpentine river below. This stone whose rough ridges I caress centers my life, a hub for all the trails undulating from this path that I have walked in all seasons. With whom? How many? Dare I conjure them all? "Who would have thought death had undone so many?"

Changes finally noted jolt me to the living present: a forest glade and meadow cut away replaced by chain link fence. The steep stony path that dropped away, once always a challenge, now gone. When all this seemed new, and most of us were young beyond our years, we made our way carefully down this steep rocky path through a grassy glade to the yellow sandbar by the swift green river. So caught up were we in self-importance and our discourse, all so properly attired in tweed, linen, and cravat, our uniform that displayed our social obligation, we hardly noted how the path narrowed from rock and dirt, thinned to a dark line of trampled grass, then cut beneath tall brush that rose above our heads. Now my attire signifies no social difference from those who ignore my admonition ambling on ahead in chattering clumps dressed in jeans, jersey, sweatshirt, men with hair worn long down around their shoulders.

Across the valley, structures shaped from slivers of trees, shaked and shingled, slowly dominate the steep bluff. On the highway below, once a killing road, the steady passing autos, eighteen wheelers promoted needed change. The road widened, now instead of people crushed by steel, trees and ferns wither from noxious fumes.

Ancient towering trees above now open to slate gray sky letting in dulled light, their bark so thick and gnarled they bear the accidental hollows dug by gnawing beast. Once a dim green hush, a stillness made even more so by small, quick movements and twitterings birds, rustlings of other creatures safely hidden, these red brown trunks of trees in endless rows of disarray close in the sky, the forest floor thick with fern and bush and moss and leafy decay that nest vibrant coils of slithering serpents, a mass I almost step on climbing over rotting limbs of trees fallen long ago.

Once upon a time walking here alone I met a bearded man on the downward slope of his prime who fled the phantoms of his past pursuing him through the years to this closed hushed place among the trees. His spectacles caught the soft light. "Flashbacks!" he cried. "Things coming at me through the trees! I survived the swamps of 'Nam!" "Nothing but a trained killer! I can't take this!" He had done his duty well. Now there were small phantom men in black coming from behind trees and brush to seek retribution for his past deeds.

We walked together down the damp forest path, he who suffered quilt and shame and bitter anger from zeal and love of country to destroy men whose only crime was having misplaced dreams of peace and love and life similar to his. ("Dulce et decorum est pro patria mori").

We made our way back to the warm safety of structures awarded for design with vinyl floors and chrome fixtures, plastic knives and forks and spoons, paper cups and plates, food prepared in an instant served warm. We lost each other among the host of vibrant, heated bodies dressed in current fashion quivering to thunderous chords that passed for song, raucous cries, screaming atonal replacement for hallelujah choirs."

# Poetry Reading

At first you think
    You're at a fashion show
    the way they parade before us
    with their words,
    the gritty detail
    of their lives
    their poems a paradox
    or oxymoron—
    self-conscious humility
    sometimes arrogant
    So we sell ourselves—
    our souls
    bidding for fame
    or love
    offering words that once released
    become confession
    Bartering our lives
    we strike a deal:
    Treat us as kindly
    as you would an animal
    caged
    released
    wary
    newly free

# 47 Degrees North
## Aftermath

The sleeping warmth beside me
    The glow within
    Beyond the shaded window pane
    Mute on clinging leaves still green
    Small on gravel darkening
    Dull upon the soggy lawn
    Soft autumn rain
    Steeps the spent dawn

# Crows and seagulls

lift
    swirl mingle
    in the sweet
    still quickening
    before dawn
    Scolding me
    in raucous chorus
    seagulls screal
    in soft rain
    that steeps
    dumb blind buildings
    Sweet rain
    cleansing me
    anoints
    the burgeoning
    slow extruding
    quiet resurrection
    of the day

# Contemplation

That tree
    whose quiet thrust
    endures against
    such perfect blue
    soars silent
    reaching darkness
    gathering
    starlight
    in leaves
    whose palisades
    absorb
    diffuse
    transpire
    the universe—
    A holiness of green

# Arboretum

Even in their dying
     things of this world
     have their brief beauty
     The bright red leaf
     that sounds my heart
     pales darkens
     fibers drying
     lose their hold
     the dead leaf
     plunges
     to
     rain-blanched
     earth

# Dependency

Dark mornings when small
   sudden fleeing summer rain
   ends too brief a wash
   of early autumn leaves,
   I, too, seek comfort
   in habit avoiding events
   pursuing me that drive
   me to a search for safe
   dry burrows in which
   to settle and savor
   the quilted warmth
   of contact from soft
   yellow light and latticed
   windows framing red bark
   cedar, speckled alder,
   and I relish the drum
   and rush and guttering
   rain on roofs and remnant
   leaves winnowing in
a chilled dismal dawn

# Raptor

Beneath the green of red bark hemlock
a quiet cove with glint of scattered bone
clean of flesh, one sinuous spinal curve
among scattered flakes of soiled feathers
High above at the peak of ancient tree
the shrill shriek of raptor
its stark white head as glorious
as the dump of bones far below
beneath its high jumbled nest
How fitting the fierce glaring eye
hooked beak curved talon
our nation's emblem.

# The Bounty

The weathered tree in my front yard
    bears annual fruit withstanding years
    of gnarled rotted limbs hoary with moss
    One winter from the hollow
    that in another year held a pool
    of clear rainwater to quench
    the thirst of small quick birds
    small mushrooms
    issued on slender stalks
    Each year thin knotty stems
    seek the sky aspiring toward sunlight
    blossoming in glorious splendor
    pink, white, and green
    scattering in the warming breeze
    issuing succulent fruit
    that satisfies a host
    of seasonal beasts—
    ants—wasps—birds—me
    Most that it bears drops
    to the ground startling cats
    crouched among branches
    coveting birds, spoiled produce
    I gather in boxes I send off to feed a bull.
    But now and then I find one globe
    inviolate, unbruised, unbored
    by winged or wandering beast
    long gone to forage other gardens
    Eating such singular fruit
    of this enduring tree a primal blessing
    unsanctioned, unsanctified, unpunished

what need then for another tree
condemning us to be like greedy gods
that curse us in their jealous anger?

# Poet's Choice
# The Garden

where she sucked upon the fruit
    while the serpent wound
    His dazzling form so smooth
    the rich fruit dropped
    she sunk
    to darkening earth
    her head
    went back
    upon the bright clean grass
    her hissing tongue
    wet her parted lips
    the moist snake coiled
    and
    held
    her thrashing hips
    while she cried out
    in new unnatural joy
    of love, of life,
    of coming death

# Rondo on Blue Paper

The sea
    of empty paper waiting
    like the earth
    waiting
    like the empty sky waiting
    like my life
    waiting like
    The sea

# Poet's Choice

Shape
defines the discipline
for shape imposes limitation:
words figures movements twist together
to a string thread back upon themselves
spread again toward their dimension
return to weave
a fabric
until
the pattern
speaking for itself
commands attention
and words are lost
light blends with movement
figures dominate reflecting life
made orderly by
shape

# Pavane for a Dead Prince

The years—
>dark wood around the door
>soul groping
>bitter hard despair
>The many years—
>a last bright day alone
>afraid helplessly aware
>of the sadness in his wail
>his knowing look
>as he cries
>So many years—
>thick living grass
>soft winds
>stir pine boughs
>bright heads of flowers
>blossoming
>Too many years—
>turning from
>that black void
>gouged from vibrant earth
>toward a radiant star
>that brings warm mist
>soft buds swelling on twigs
>thin green blades fusing
>through barren earth
>to fill the world
>with wonder

# Words for Pascal's Dervish

To him
　His flesh
　was thick and strong
　firm and full
　with heat and blood
　above the round rich vessels
　of his life
　Yet
　In the quiet of the stars
　His flesh
　was just
　a fragile slender reed
　against the dark night

# Study—3

My word-child
    Oh, child
    of my dark mind
    why all the pain
    to bear you
    to the light
    upon
    a barren
    page?
    Oh, child
    wet quiverings of my brain
    when finally
    you rip
    from night
    why all
    the
    red
    blood
    spilled?
    Black
    earth
    soaks
    deep
    rich
    with
    life

# Study—4

Night
    I alone beneath the tree
    with long leaves hanging
    fragrant moist
    silent in their stir
    until the warm balmy
    breeze ceases
    to let the still
    night stand

# Study—5

```
all i was
    ashes
    wisps
    rising
    in steam
    bringing
    sweet
    remembrances
    vanishing
```

# Study—8

Overhead
    Keening voices in the tree
    Reach down through darkness
    To find me deep in shadows
    From overhead the image
    creeps through darkness
    to find my bones
    white and dry
    whispering
    from the dark pit

# Pantoum—1

Brief gifts of moments
    clung to as a child
    cling to us later
    our lingering grief
    clung to as a child
    our days of joy
    our lingering grief
    our nights of sorrow
    our days of joy
    so bright so fleeting
    our nights of sorrow
    our endless waking
    so bright so fleeting
    sunlight and clouds
    our endless waking
    when grief returns

# Pantoum—2

Love the web
    strong delicate
    as gossamer thread
    a slow deliberate spider fashions
    Strong delicate
    the tactile net
    a slow deliberate spider fashions
    to snag the unsuspecting
    the tactile net
    billowing in the wind
    to snag the unsuspecting
    thrums with vibrant life held fast
    Billowing in the wind
    the delicate deliberate web
    thrums with vibrant life held fast
    until the spider descends

# Pantoum—3

The web of passion
    a tactile net
    of gossamer thread
    the slow deliberate spider fashions
    A tactile net
    strong deliberate
    the slow deliberate spider fashions
    to snag the unsuspecting
    Strong deliberate
    billowing in the wind
    to snag the unsuspecting
    thrums with a vibrant life held fast
    Billowing in the wind
    the gossamer web
    thrums with a vibrant life held fast
    until the spider descends

# Villanelle

My love, my life, my endless passion—you
    sound my soul with joy and sorrow
    the single moment of my life that's true
    Sometimes as radiant as each new sun
    my love is warmed with each tomorrow
    my love, my life, my endless passion—you
    in moments bless the nights when I like someone who
    with waning strength beyond what I can borrow
    the single moment of my life that's true
    plunge to that pit from which no person ever drew
    salvation nor could save himself from all the sorrow
    of my love my life, my endless passion—you
    I know how you have lived the anguish too
    from so much hope all dreams will be redeemed tomorrow
    from my love, life, endless passion—you
    the single moment of my life that's true

# Mea Culpa

Someday
    I'll write a poem
    about those things
    mechanical
    that every time—
    interjections to my serious thought—
    become like pins, fine laserings
    that sting and prick
    my swelled pretensions
    I know
    Each time I use them,
    quick catches of my reeling mind—
    the squish, the gel,
    the quivering nerve,
    the gnash of teeth, mat of hair,
    the clamorous bone—
    Those tools—
    appendages of messy flesh—
    compel a stumbling
    stammering
    humility renewed
    my rediscovery is this—
    How will I climb limb over limb
    above myself to places rich
    from expectation?
    How will my thoughts
    (compressed like aerosol)
    release to mist
    to spray to disinfect
    protect to hiss and rise and fill

the world
this ripe, mammalian room
with scent of angels
disguising odors
reeking of my sentiment?
I fail
I falter
fumble—
hands
all fingers
two large opposing thumbs
that hook in gears
my flesh forever
snatched in synchromesh

# Saunterings
# Mexican Bus Ride

The mountains drove us to the sky
    beyond the clouds so that the blue
    distant peaks as we ascended
    broke through like islands far below
    All gasped chattering
    laughing with excitement
    in a language
    only recently falteringly mine
    All joined in hallelujah chorus
    all except El Viego at my side
    so tanned so shrunk he seemed
    as still as dirt or death gazing
    from the heaven to which we
    had been heaved by our prayers
    and chortling bus
    From Mazatlan'
    he had broken with me my bread
    And now he shared with me
    beneath his breath
    the prayer he offered
    praise wonderment or fear
    mumbled on the rosary
    of rubber band he stretched
    twirling it in gnarled twisted hands
    Then we descended:
    Each town we came through
    across the flat, starlit desert night
    he spoke its name as if it held

a magic or a mystery only
he could bear: Durango, Saltillo,
Torreon, where we arrived at dawn
And I descended
wrinkled shrunk cramped
following him
his brief vaya con dios
as he scuttled off
hurrying past the old cathedral
through the slowly gathering
market crowd captured
in the holy aura
of a new golden light

# View from the Great Pyramid
## at Chichen-itza'

Here at the margin of the world
    raised in this place above the flat
    rich plain of sea-green jungle that runs
    until the earth bends, the mind ends,
    where men left monuments outlasting flesh,
    their bones and spirits lingering,
    I imagine myself much like a voyager,
    some soul stranded on an island
    in a vast wild waste, or like him
    aboard that first ship with nothing
    but the dark fathomless blue below,
    the sky above with billowing clouds
    that sail full-blown before the gulf-wind
    never lingering
    How he must have felt alone
    in full command shaping his world,
    the ship he steers wrenched
    from the wounded earth,
    hacked, hewn, sealed against wind,
    rain, tide, and acrid fear of men
    more terrified than he facing himself
    Alone like that, he has the need
    to judge and rule himself,
    more than he or anyone
    thought possible, despite
    the praise, the prophecy,
    the acclamation, and the power
    he alone with only cloud, sea, sky,

knows one world, that one world his
Now here below
people blackened by the sun
appear from paths to some place
who knows where their world begins
in empty huts with hammocks
packed earth floors, pigs, chickens,
bawling, laughing children
Nothing else in this green 'desert
devouring monuments of stone piled
on sculptured stone once reaching
to seize the ripe, dark force
that finally drowned them
in an endless wild.
Where then the stake
or sculptured stone
to anchor dream
or hope or pious faith?

# On Top the Great Pyramid
# at Chichen-itza'

Close ancient room
    Fluttering frenzied forms
    with odors almost human leave
    droppings on the packed earth floor
    Lice in sunlight edge the dark interior
    Each step I take alone I flay myself
    contending with black ghostly shapes
    from the past that that fling
    themselves at me then soar
    again fleeing to safety
    within a dark vault of mute
    stone worn ageless
    cleansed by the sun
    the blood of holy sacrifice
    and willing victim

# On the Way to the Ball Court at Chichen-itza'

Whether
    existential choice
    or irony of chance
    toppled stones
    once
    a Temple of Warriors
    lie scattered
    among vines

# On the Esplanade at Chichen-itza'

The link
    between that time and this,
    even though the unfamiliar tongue
    I stumble on seems just as foreign here
    sacrificial virgins still help men
    expelled finally from the womb
    acclaim themselves:
    The promenade—
    a man behind
    a woman gorged with child,
    his—we presume—
    his hand around her neck
    as if she wore a chain
    while others pass mirroring his pose:
    the comb through slick raven hair
    the settled hats
    the spit to prove they still have seed
    to guard against ancient myths
    of pale ghosts who challenge them
    emasculating them from a glance
    at their possession those women
    who study me admitting
    more than what they reveal
    in confession

# Leaving Merida

Fat forms laboring to be men
    in gray uniforms almost as blue
    as musk on ripe plums strained
    to bursting halt
    The gathering morning heat
    with pink light creeping
    from the jungle splays
    the plaza and the crumbling
    ancient church
    as two in bleached print
    non-regulation shirt
    faded pants, scuffed shoes
    their only dress are singled out
    Thin ones old too soon
    their dreams of glory
    long betrayed
    their rebellion long dead
    yet almost pleased
    (faint serious smile)
    at being drilled:
    un! ... dos! ... un! dos! ...
    guida atras' to win attention
    while others watch at rest
    as I march by
    in perfect cadence
    learned from the blood

# Leaving Merida—2

They marched me out of town
    those men in Merida who drilled
    to music then were gone behind
    the crumbling adobe church
    their lively music carrying them
    away as I left keeping their time
    following my all too human heritage
    of lofty pyramids buried beneath
    sea green jungle and blazing sun
    in Yucatan

# The Sewerage Problem at Versailles

Now no following violins
    attached to men
    Now no voices in the air
    to please the royal ear
    Now no suitors woo
    the royal hand
    Now the silence
    n among the trees
    still pruned
    the shimmering leaf
    and sun-bleached pebbles
    undisturbed
    Now the walks so silent
    in the sun are free
    Yet even now
    the lingering scent
    of blooming orange trees
    fills the ravaged air

# Agnostic

Blind voices
    Chant the dark dirge
    Until the drone lulls
    My drowsed soul
    To dulled acceptance
    But then—
    My god!
    Such dumb devotion
    Staggers my mind
    Stumbling
    To numbed awareness
    While
    Those cloaked voices
    Never change
    Their sound
    Ascending
    Echoing
    Rising
    Persisting
    Praising
    God

# Tourist

We came from sunlight
    to thick walled darkness
    cool moist hushed
    and reverent
    Compelled
    we whispered
    fell to stone-dumb silence
    heard the echo
    ring the chant
    undaunted
    by our sceptical
    intrusion
    Until
    that hallowed body
    sounded to the haunted hollow
    that took the constant cry
    and stirred the Virgin's window
    sending back praise
    raised on high

# Venice

Santa Maria Della Salute's
   Glorious ivory dome swells
   from the waters of the Grand Canal
   bristling with red, white, blue
   barber poles and black gondolas
   beside the great wide walkway
   sweeping in a grand yellow curve
   toward the Campanile, Doge's Palace,
   Bridge of Sighs beneath a pale blue
   Mediterranean sky as if we were walking
   into a Canaletto painting rediscovering
   perspective
   Dark passageways, small dark compos
   In the warm night, a stout woman leaning
   on the rail of her venetian balcony
   discoursing with another stout woman
   in the compo below, her venetian tongue
   cracks the black veil of heavy humid air
   Across from our hotel the façade of the church
   speckled white with dripping pigeon dung,
   where Vivaldi once led and orchestra
   of young women closeted from wealthy
   families playing his one melody
   of a thousand variations, sharp whistles,
   raucous cries of young gorged venetian
   men below calling above to young
   American women ripe for exploitation
   The elegant splendor of a quiet green garden,
   The pink Guggenheim palazzo, wrought iron
   fixtures along the canal, postcard picture twisted

columns and Romanesque windows.
Oh! To be so blessed with so much
wealth living in indolent indulgence
beside fetid green waters of the great lagoon
from which Santa Maria Della Salute's
glorious dome rises in antique splendor
In the church of John and Paul
sacred murals in the dim holy light
the sacristan offers us with a quick flick
of a switch, the walls and ceiling bursting
into splendid pastel blues and reds above
the gray slate stones that cap the crypt
of Veronese floating in a watery grave,
a wrinkled embryo waiting eternally
for resurrection

# View from Coit Tower

At the margin of our world
    The angel of the Gate
    Flames into fading light
    Upon the pines beneath us
    While behind us
    Our proud captain
    His armored chest ballooned
    Searches, seizes, forges
    A world rising to meet us
    In the darkening Bay
    Where
    Solid in the water
    Pestered by pleasure craft
    Alcatraz winks back
    Signaling Columbus
    Of his success regaining paradise

# State Fair in Sacramento

Madonna in pink dress
    with dark hair, dark humid eyes
    as deep as summer night
    as heavy as the fragrant, peeling trees
    beyond the carnival where colored light
    seeps among eucalyptus
    Madonna of pale skin,
    sharp, thin features, ripened belly,
    your head drooped slightly to one side
    Madonna of the tired eyes
    in whose arms the child sleeps
    lost to the hot lights, shrill cries
    that leap from whirling rides,
    safe from the sweating sticky host
    that streams on all sides
    Our Lady of dark, glazed eyes
    raising specters of Cervantes,
    lovely, quiet Andelusian gardens,
    the red, wet fury of la corrida de toros,
    and she lost in sweet dreams
    deaf and mute to the toothless woman
    at your side: La Vieja in worn, faded dress,
    soiled scarf, stiff, gray hair, furrowed face,
    sunken, mouth, dangling cigarette smoking
    to her squinting eyes as she takes the sleeping
    child and leaves you settle into soft peace
    Sweet Lady. Gaze with El Greco,
    your world, stigmatic, blurred, beautiful,
    and new letting the ancient woman
    at your side beat her gums,

her constant yammering faith enough
to hold against the endless carnival of night

# Creation by Design

(in our own image)
    Cool morning air
    As we move in a slow
    Caravan toward the interstate
    Passing ranches
    Nestled in the grooves
    Of green hills rounded
    From the wear of endless seasons
    Cows of various breed and color
    Graze in green pastures
    Later, as the sun warms
    The golden hills mowed of grain
    We flash by Calistoga
    In early summer heat
    First the fetid stench we anticipate
    Then the panoramic vista
    As far as we can view
    Multitudes of cattle
    Feeding in tranquility
    Along endless troughs
    Docile creatures
    Masticating quietly
    In black brown barren turf
    Churned by four hooves
    Of every beast
    Designed for slaughter
    While we flash by
    For at least three miles
    At eighty miles per hour
    Farther up the pot-holed road

Vast signboards promote
Our next meal of steak
With all the trimmings
That will later decompose
To organic waste
We will excrete
Cover and mask
By means of various
Cosmetic scents
Disguising our earthly nature
Promoting our auspicious aspirations

# Encounters
# Clytemnestra

I snared him in his bath while he soaked,
    the warm, scented water steeping his guilt,
    leaving him exposed, self-righteous, smug,
    deflecting blame—fate had wrestled him
    to his wretched burden, his duty to his kin
    Yet, how his loins had churned for war
    lusting for battle, just as he pursued
    those he took as slaves, his gorged flesh
    a sword that made the slaughter richer
    still as he pressed into them, forcing them
    to take his spent seed, sowing his heritage
    No, not in defense of homeland
    but for false, bloody, ransom,
    for betrayal of a woman whose man
    could not hold her, he, too, pursuing
    the spoiling of flesh, his seed spilling
    in ruined, unwilling vessels,
    their spirit fleeing willing violation
    Then the greatest horror! His monstrous
    indifference to her cries as he ravished
    every virtue, all that was pure! My child—
    his own daughter—his offering to fickle
    gods never satisfied, their craving for piety
    reflected in our feckless need for power
    My revenge came sweet with rage
    wrenched from the wounded earth,
    hammered to a burnished blade
    that pierced his flesh, opening gaping

mouths, destroying precious, living harmony,
leaving the curse of death for me
at the mercy of the son I bore
on the birth bed of pain, conceived
not in love but in luck, obeying again
the legacy of gods who mock
our fragile human goodness

# Thais

Alexander fights for conquest, lusts for fame.
    Thais waits in the tent on the hill.
    Who then is the conqueror?
    Thais, whose mortal merits seep in sifting sand,
    faceless, featureless in time, her name as lasting
    as the slowly crumbling pyramids even after flesh
    is gone and only bones then finally only desert
    sand remains under distant stars
    Thais, strong legs and thighs bringing
    her from Athens through hot sand, starry nights
    south to the Valley of the Nile then deep into Babylon
    following Alexander, those legs and thighs
    dark from many suns, quiet now in cool water
    brought from a well by those standing guard
    at unsealed tent flaps, men gorged with blood
    as her slender hands caress the water soon
    to stroke a strong hard back.
    Thais in the tent, thin garments brush her legs,
    her thighs, relax, anticipate the night inviting
    Alexander to rest from the sweating grit of battle
    throughout the long day beneath dazzling sky
    fighting, fighting, fighting for the whole world
    and all that comes along with it for the taking
    Thais waiting while he bathes, eats, quaffs wine.
    Within the tent beneath the stars
    low whispers, quick movements, soft cries
    muffled by tent wall while outside
    smoking fire, crackling wood, roasting meat,
    a sentry listening clears his throat, shifts his weight,
    aches for the long night to pass exposing

the town lying open before him in the dawn
when fires glimmer and the sky glows red
over the blue black distant hills.

# A Poem For Sancho

Saints and men alike, perhaps
    sometimes take fat forms.
    I
    First they make him island governor
    and he, amazed at his ascension,
    found justice difficult
    So he mimicked Solomon
    until they came for him shouting
    and he in grubby underwear
    confused by dreams, their mocking cries,
    their burning torches
    went with them into the night
    Where jammed
    in heavy icy shields
    he twirled,
    spun,
    fell
    his face in mud
    Men shouted milling
    drums, gunshots, torches whirled
    around him in the night
    When he gaped at them
    they stomped on him
    pressed him into muddy
    ripened earth

II

Their laughter dwindled with the flares
    The night, the torches bled to dawn
    They took him up, wiped him clean
    gave him wine, set him in his bed
    "It's dawn," he said.
    He gazed out at the blue mist of hills
    He rose to dress
    and once again in worn smelly clothes
    he asked for nothing
    only bread, a little cheese,
    some barley for his animal
    he swung astride, left with what he came,
    disappeared without a backward glance
    They watched him as he rode away
    his fat frame swaying humorous and sad
    while turning back toward private lives
    recalled his parting words that he would
    rather have liberty beneath an oak
    then all the power of government

138

# III

Under the tree
>he sat with a long lost friend refound
>An empty wine skin lay between
>Flies buzzed
>While he slept in shade
>Dapple grazed
>head hung
>near

# For Lorca

Federico, mi amigo mio
    You could not even in your wild
    imagining mind imagine me
    sitting here thinking of you then
    For now I know at last your fear has ended
    For now I know you finally met the dark shadow
    of your skull that always troubled you
    Now I know for you there is no light
    Now I know the skies for you are empty skies
    Federico, tell me what your mind imagined
    when they took you out beneath your wide blue
    summer skies with high white clouds that sailed
    before the lazy breeze when they stood you up
    against your own dark trees with yellow leaves
    and darkness came with bits of biting steel
    when you fell
    Federico, mi amigo mio
    Rest in dark peace somewhere

# Newsreel: Nativity

A woman falters
    jolting unborn
    life stumbling
    through
    dull clatter
    of tumbling brick
    Bitter wind rattles
    shattered family
    portraits dangling
    from jagged debris
    Dead buried under walls
    Dogs search snuffling
    under rubble
    wi nd pil es snow
    revealing black frozen earth
    While within
    wet darkness
    where no walls fall
    as fast as men bleeding
    summer days
    under sheltering trees
    Life drips time
    until from
    soft gurgling
    repose—
    a chil d

# On Aggression

We probe each other in the mind
    rear back and raise a slender bold
    presuming staff
    against another heart's desire
    or fall then yield
    offering mucus, flesh,
    or stirring dream
    drawing in the probing reed
    ferreting to find
    our hidden darkness

# Original Sin: Pledge Allegiance

The Chinese and the Russians
      have it too this grave disease
      called humanness. Chronic bickering,
      malignant quarrels make these wars
      holy and faith internalized,
      iatric zeal transmogrifies the soul:
      The ripened seed hides
      in the fruit its own decay
      The image is not clear:
      The photograph bled through
      transmission becomes a painting:
      On the icy plain a small group
      at the right thick with padding
      moves armed toward center
      almost as if turning
      from the alien line
      of darker figures to the left
      l imagine then a sudden,
      sharp exchange of words,
      weapons whipped in reflex
      from shoulders stutter shocks,
      hot explosions on the winter air,
      while men, still surprised,
      slump, sag
      Silence brings conjecture:
      Surely they had conjured this
      Surely they expected this,
      Prophesying this in some
      old cave or wooden barracks
      maintained by number

Yet even at this distance
I can see the awe of those
who creep to bend
and gaze upon the twitching
dead
The old clichés arise—
they, too, have photos
captured in the purse
with images that smile
in frozen scene and wait
for those congealing on
the cold Siberian plain
until returned:
Then the sacks that
once held symptoms,
chronic signs of humanness,
sink toward remnants
of the Sinanthropus,
who, I hear, broke neighboring bones
to suck their marrow
The soil returns
Time leeches petty detail
Dark hollows fill the void
Memory chills then gels
With sentiment at public funerals

# Boot Camp

When young and even more foolish
    fulfilling my patriotic duty
    pro patria mori
    I was always one drafted for KP
    because I always asked questions
    ignoring the often cited dictum:
    "Yours is not to reason why
    yours is but to do or die"
    What I was supposedly patrolling
    has always been unclear
    save that I burnished
    scorched pots and pans
    to gleaming metal
    or skimmed floating
    vomit scum from grease traps
    beneath metal sinks
    Roused from sleep before reveille
    assigned to night watch shivering
    in the chill pre-dawn air
    I stoked and tended kitchen fires
    choking on sooty coal smoke
    waiting for morning muster
    and the line of bodies entering
    to pass while I ladled heaps on
    metal plates on metal trays I later
    cleaned along with various utensils
    in the rush of running faucet
    after all the stoked bodies
    filed out to do their duty
    Finished just before midday chow

I crept off seeking solace
in my empty bunk
lounging on the brown
blanket so taut a coin would bounce,
my dogged feet in combat boots
hung from the edge while I dozed
until a strident voice ordered
me rise move quickstep
back to Augean labors
never fully done
How long ago that dismal scene
I choose not to recall
but those times consistently
redeemed by equally strident
commands from a hausfrau
who never ceases to find chores
to interrupt the stumbling
faltering construction of a poem

# Poems upon Occasions
## A Poem for All Occasions

So small, so few
    these fragile words,
    reminding me
    of yellow flowers
    speckled brown,
    soft, still,
    feeble in their hold on time.
    I thought at first
    I'd send you flowers—
    yellow flowers
    specked brown
    Yet all I have are words
    to fill this day
    with quiet thoughts:
    Rays of morning sunlight
    streaming down through clouds
    yellow flowers
    beside still water
    underneath budding trees
    green with love

# Secular Prayer

May my dream
    never die
    may my love
    always glow
    as the bright
    star of morning
    bright star
    of evening
    May this song
    find its way
    on quick wings
    of the dove
    strong wings
    of the gull
    to the mountains
    the sea beneath
    billowing clouds
    to my love

# In Praise of Courtly Love

Dante
> With his Beatrice
> Has nothing on me
> Nor is
> Petrarch's Laura
> More than she
> My Lady

# Nonce on a Theme by Williams

This is
    just to say
    I have
    helped
    myself
    to the silence
    and pleasure
    of your lingering scent
    hung with your soft clothes
    the hushed air
    the lonely fern
    the hallowed room
    spare in provisions
    the stir and dull thump
    from other dwellings
    the fresh muffin
    its sweet surprise
    the quiet joy
    of haunted sharing

# The Dance

We move together
hearing our own melody.
We turn in harmony,
part, reach, touch, fuse again,
our movements in measures
of emotion upon a scale
that plunges us toward
inner light and whirls us
to a secret core
Our being fills
a universe
of
self-consuming
stars

# Sanctuary

A holy place: those fields
    of ripened wheat that fan
    in sweeping waves beneath
    the quilted shadows
    of the clouds
    You hide there from the world
    of angry, drunken fathers
    indifferent mothers. You shy
    from corn rows with host
    of hard-shelled, winged beasts
    and weaveled spume
    Then with the blue scar of sky
    above, you hug your soul
    reveling in the sunbaked
    fragrances of earth and grain,
    closed in, secure, the picketing
    fence of wheat stalks at your face
    before your eyes as bright
    and clear as crystal
    Safe in that primal forest,
    filled with a joy of freedom
    where no one will ever find you
    you listen in the endless hush
    of sunlight, of stirring wheat
    for the voice forever searching
    forever answered by the sweet
    sudden exultation of the lark

# Taking Leave

All things true must
     end, if not love itself
     then just those moments
     shaped from imperfection:
     A fine jade bowl
     carved with care
     more than what was
     spent on love
     A silk scroll of irises
     suspended in the hush
     of a hallowed room
     There the groping struggle
     ends, no need for words.
     The spirit of this room
     steeps and fills the soul
     offering however brief
     a moment's pause.
     So it's finished, then,
     hard to bear.
     Harder still the absent
     touch, the lingering scent
     of love's sweet flowering.
     Gone, too, the probe
     the plunge, the final
     surge and break
     leaving lovers spent
     resting in each other's
     arms lost in those
     separate dreams beyond
     all words all thoughts

no one can ever cage
not even in a bowl,
a scroll, or faltering poem.
Hardest of all
those seven wretched years
we fought each other's
sick imaginings leaving
emptiness as deep as loss
of one brief child
who gasped her life
away and we no longer
share bed, board, weariness,
or pain, all gone
as suddenly as life,
the grief as deep
and lasting as the death
of one accidental child.

# Epiphanies
## Silence

is full of noises:
    fly buzz
    through an empty room
    Heater hum
    softly
    while I end my song
    Sounds
    through window panes
    bring sunlight
    flowers
    engines gasoline
    on fire—
    Explosions internal
    match mine

# Through a Glass Darkly

Bright leaves,
    scattered leaves,
    a galaxy
    that spirals
    the dark
    occasional pool
    appearing
    after
    heavy rain
    Now
    I
    occasional
    a quiet pool
    formed from dark earth
    define the fallen leaves:
    red leaves
    revealing drying veins
    yellow leaves
    remnants of the sun
    hidden now
    by clouds
    Rain
    upon the dirt-streaked
    window
    feels
    no
    pain

# The Vision
## (Theme)

The twilight gathers
    And the distant mountains
    Deepen toward the night
    The twilight gathers
    While the rich red wine
    Gathers in my blood
    Numbs my mind
    Against the twilight
    And shimmer of fading
    Light along the mountains
    The twilight fails
    While wine flows
    With music swelling
    Through the darkening house
    And when the music throbs
    My numbed soul
    Becomes a sound rich with pain
    That spills me full
    Stunned by twilight
    Splits the black earth
    And spills the crumbling coffin
    With leached-white bones

# (Variation)

From overhead
    the keening in the fir
    reaches down
    to find me
    deep in shadow
    From overhead
    the image
    seeps through darkness
    to find my bones
    white and dry whispering
    from the dark pit

# Fortunate Flaw

Words faltering fail.
    The beauty of the world
    Endures.
    I
    die

# Burial

So

you won
My beard is gone
Each anniversary of my death
plumb my grave
to shave
me

# Song

Poetry is such a perfect
   way of healing pain
   world wounds
   until from bitter
   darkness my heart
   sings such joyous
   sounds
   of sweet discovery:
   Pain wrings
   the glory from my soul

# Jumbo

Jet plane soaring overhead
    wide silver wings spread
    engines baffling in a rushing
    whirling sucking roar of screaming
    metal that can only be a jumbo
    compelling me to strain back
    gazing after as it climbs
    That ripping raging roar
    and glorious soaring image
    conjures a locomotive horn
    at night or in blue back dawn
    its long wail always resurrecting
    glistening tracks running
    parallel to the horizon
    the long dopplered moan
    stirring up places far away
    far beyond the point
    where tracks converge
    disappear at last
    beyond the beyond

# Caboose

Sometimes rust red
    trailing on after chasing
    fleeing rocking cars
    bringing up the rear
    as always
    its image growing smaller
    smaller
    smaller
    until the long glistening
    blue black line of tracks
    oil-stained wood sleepers
    grimy gravel
    rise up before us
    restoring us to the world

# Secular Saints
## Descartes in Stockholm

What bitter cold. He had not felt such cold
    since that one time before. He hated cold,
    avoided cold, just as he shunned labor.
    His work was mind. So he thought rising
    in the dark on winter mornings, the night
    lingering. No rational man would choose
    such a living: the heavy coat of fur
    in which he buried himself could not suffice.
    He would rather be in bed surveying
    the scrolled ceiling calculating vectors
    until the sun at its zenith warmed him.
    But here now in this hellish place
    the rime frost graveled walk glimmering
    in the blue gray light of dawn cracked
    beneath his well-turned shoe
    because the young queen commanded:
    Her mind craved the clarity of dawn
    before the light, her passion for the truth
    offsetting her unreasonable demands.
    How well he imagined himself like her
    traveling the distance in time and space
    to the warm oven where he had crawled
    escaping the long Bavarian winter to ponder
    mysteries that suddenly had burdened him
    with doubt. Yet the priests had taught him well:
    The old beliefs well-fixed, the new science
    based on mathematics swelled in him like yeast
    Such youthful optimism: enthused, he seized

the paradox that doubt would ransom all:
Seeking first what was simple, clear, distinct
on pain of contradiction, from these basic truths
he could restore faith: The world fell into his hands.
But that was long ago, so distant. Here, now,
in this place that God, himself, it seemed, had forsook
the chill northern damp steeped his very soul
as he hurried away toward the lesson, the slight catch
in his throat, the tightness in his chest made him cough.
Yet once in her presence, tall, blond, youthful,
what a woman she was, how grand she would be,
her energy of thought, her challenges and claims
would sweep him along, heating him until dismissed
into the lung-stinging air. Such yielding
to intemperance shunning reason exacted its price:
Three days later he was dead.

# Spinoza at the Hague

From the south dark
        summer clouds above steep
        ancient roofs bring warm
        rain with rings in canals
        like glass arcs he grinds,
        slivers of spheres
        while contemplating substance
        and the nature of faith,
        his thought so patient,
        as delicate as deliberate
        as the glide and rhythm
        of his work while he slowly
        polishes making them more fine:
        Evil seems to be
        the nature of the world.
        He knows from experience:
        Iberian transplant Jew,
        persecution, cruelty, endless
        disasters, natural and human,
        all these his heritage.
        Yet all is for the best:
        "The world is one—
        ergo, one with God.
        The world and God
        are one—ergo, there is
        no God. Or – what joy –
        God is everywhere!
        I am, God, God, me!"
        But this climate grows too rare.
        He must breathe. His finite

body, a marvelous machine,
must haul the burden of his soul,
that mystery. Rich blood
must course through locks
and channels creating paradox:
sweet life's fine residue,
a universe of microcosmic
spheres crowding minute vesicles
grinding them, that marvelous
mechanism, God's splendid
handiwork responds: finite flesh
in compensation swells,
the cybernetic cycle holds
consuming him, reducing him
first to mind, then to substance,
then to God

# Kant in Konigsberg

Immanuel gazed at the distant tower.
        that steeple digging inward daily toward a priori
        burrowing into his mind defining for him once
        and for all our limited consciousness
        But, then, a fortiori, the thin, young tree,
        scrawnier than he, postulated twigs,
        axiomatic buds induced perennially,
        unfurling heuristic leaves
        at the certain change of seasons
        when winter light warmed,
        those wondrous engines by so reaching,
        argued, aspired, imposed themselves,
        obscuring from Immanuel the steeple
        and its unfelt, unrational
        indication of our tacit hope.
        "Can't! Can't! Ought not do that!"
        Kant cried.
        Thus, he objected.
        Thus spoke.
        So the pious city fathers hacked down
        that burgeoning tree to satisfy the need
        and human longing of that little man,
        the town great's attraction by whom they
        set their clocks upon his daily walk.
        He may as well have sliced them
        with his words those forceful limbs
        so that his harsh pruning might
        clear his thought as necessary and sufficient
        as his proclaimed reasoning cleared for us
        forever more our sensuous air.

# John Stuart Mill at Avignon

The end of life is happiness.
So it seems—at last—these days he spends
near her. Spring again: the earth renewed
with fragrances and verdant life. Flowers blossom
by her grave in the garden near the cottage
he has built to be near her where she lies.
He had known her for twenty years,
the only other soul to give him strength
to guide his life, finally asking for her hand,
once he had proved himself after he had prospered.
No surprise since few had his advantage;
fewer still returned it with such charity:
the greatest good for the greatest number.
Born to be useful, he runs his life by the clock.
Nurtured by his father's firm but liberal rule
he flourishes seated in the same room reading
Greek by three, Plato by eight, he studies
while his father writes a history of the great
sub-continent, reads economics with Ricardo,
his father's friend. Then off to that sub-continent
to work in his father's great company where he begins
as lowly clerk then through diligent work becomes director.
Along the way, he doubts his purpose:
If all his goals for government and social life
were made real, would he be happy? His answer
leads to moods from which she guides him:
An educated, well-placed man has obligations:
He should use his station and experience
for the general good of all helping those
who have no lofty standing.

He marries her at forty-five, writes works
with her that set the standard for a hundred years;
he stands for parliament where he argues
for the rights of women, fights for land reform
until she passes, when he draws upon her courage
and builds the cottage near her grave then regulates
his final spring by the memory of her certain praise.

# William James in the Adirondacks

He has everything a man could want: Old money
    gives him independence, travels in Europe
    where at the best schools he studies medicine
    but has no need to practice. Why, then, the youthful
    depression, the morbid fear that nothing will change
    the painful present, that hope is without hope?
    He decides to believe in freedom of the will, accepts
    the offer to teach the workings of the human flesh,
    contracts to write a work on the nasty little subject
    that will link the human body with elusive human mind.
    Why, then, does all his success mean so little?
    Why his days one long wrestling with something
    or with someone he couldn't see? In exchange,
    sleeplessness, digestive disorders, back pain:
    He seeks relief in European spas. Yet his disorders
    not rooted in the flesh are echoes: He fears the loss
    of self as he witnessed in one epileptic patient
    green with disease, black with dirt from whom
    he flees as augury: There but for the grace
    of chance goes he. He longs for the tranquility
    from belief. A sceptic, he postulates God
    then prays for signs, lectures on will and on faith,
    draws crowds to hear him speak on religion
    and the varieties of its experiences.
    Then the journey to the mountains where his arrival
    has been a pilgrimage, the sweet clear air
    in holy morning sunlight cleansing him,
    here where the heavens meet the solid earth
    in green peaks that stretch in waves to the horizon
    around the rough glittering rock to which he hauls

himself, at which he kneels, the core of life is revealed:
He meets the deities in an endless host. But the climb
taxes his heart, he renounces science, ignores the symptoms,
returns the following year to discover himself lost.
He collapses then is found. Carried home, he embraces
philosophy, teaches pragmatism, sails to Europe
for his body's sake, but cannot stem the flow of words.
Descanting with friends late into the night,
he despairs of relief, wears himself into submission.
With his brother Henry, he returns home for two days
then—at last— yields to an everlasting comfort of eternity.


On Denoting
    Lord Bertrand Russell
    upon a railroad bridge
    considers suicide,
    the long years without reward,
    uncertain recognition still ahead.
    Mathematics, he recalls,
    saves him.
    He sees, somehow,
    relationship
    between those forms:
    the billowing steam,
    the thundering mass
    that sweeps beneath his feet
    jarring him back to life.
    He dies
    at ninety-eight,
    strident as a gobbler,
    lean as an old, tough bird,

at home, in bed,
the nightly brandy
having warmed him
to his rest.

# Wittgenstein in Wien

He found for us our limits.
    The world, he pronounced,
    was framed in words:
    His work was finished.
    What more to say?
    That which he might have hoped
    to speak could not be said in words.
    Thus, the ladder climbed,
    he hauled it after. Now what?
    What mattered? His heritage
    meant nothing, so he renounced
    his father's legacy, lived as simply
    as a soldier or a saint, fought a private
    war in public, pondered his ideas,
    lived his belief in the trenches
    of one great war, worked
    the sick wards of another.
    Between those conflicts, his word-tight
    World turned on its head. He offered
    Himself for whatever he was worth
    Gathering to his days his meaning
    by teaching fairy tales in mountain
    hamlets, building for his wealthy sister
    a mansion as sterile as a monk's cell,
    while sitting in on but only listening
    to those descanting in the Wiener Kreise,
    (that great sausage ring of intellect)
    where he offered poetry and the large
    placard on which the single word
    he sent up like a kite that waltzes

in the Viennese spring air—
SILENCE!
He had it right. What sense in all
these words if we are led to thought
where our only hope is death by our
own hand, or in his case, the slow suck
of natural strophes. In either case,
our meaning is the same, the one
that suddenly arrives riding behind
on the same saddle as the horseman.
Should this be true, our gifts and hoard
of words or gold beggar value until spent
or squandered, cast before those we allow
to use us dreadfully who steal from us
what we would gladly yield as token
of our love or trust.
We have our fair exchange.
What more return
should we expect
from words or deeds?

# CAMUS IN SENS

He should not have made it this far.
How many times had the cosmos confronted him:
The scandal of his birthright: French cartman father,
Algerian charwoman mother, the poverty of his milieu
after his father dies; the lung-wracking disease
that all but killed him. He challenges all these blows
of fate, squinting furrow-browed through the haze
of smoke from cigarettes, his constant halo.
He learns well from Sisyphus: Life means
nothing without deeds, an absurd rock we push
up to the peak then see it tumble to the barren
plain below. The absurd walls we build around
us formed by reason: Our mind grasps anything
as real, no matter how bizarre then shapes an absurd
universe from faulty logic. Meaning lies in what we
do: resignation no matter how absurd our fate.
A person's life is like a book: We understand both
fully only after they are closed. We always
judge a person by what a person does.
Suicide is not a moral option.
His own life, just as his work, charged with irony
and chance, he works the system then wears success:
A sturdy coat of obligation: teacher, playwright,
Journalist for the French Resistance, world famous
novelist, he urges both responsibility and rebellion:
One person's right ends at the tip of another person's nose.
The Nobel Prize Committee takes notice, some how
has foresight giving the prize to one so young,
the youngest ever. With the monies he establishes
a country home outside Paris from which he leaves

one morning passing over the usual train coach
for the car ride a close friend suddenly offers.
On the highway as they speed along discoursing
on life and meaning, a rear tire slips on ice sending
them off the road against a tree. In the backseat
crushed by steel that should have saved him,
his book is finished.

# Oppenheimer at Trinity Test Site

His life plays out in three acts:
ACT ONE: The young genius nurtured on Jewish
middle-class comfort, schooled at Harvard where
he excels displaying his talents, finishing in three
quarters time what others strain to finish in four.
Fluent in five languages, he considers poetry:
French, medieval, metaphysical, in which he
would spend his years disporting at such heights.
Yet, he chooses Gottingen, studies the newest
physics, ends at Berkeley where students dread
his laser wit, lightening quick intelligence.
One student stages a hunger strike to be admitted
to his class. He finds friendship with a scholar
of French literature, a Marxist, marries a former
communist party member. Those few who know him
well call him Robert.
ACT TWO: Despite all objections to his family
and his social ties that are questionable, he is chosen,
assumes the title Director of Rapid Rupture for the project
that develops a new bomb some think impossible.
He bargains, replaying Faust: in exchange for power
that unbinds the forces of the universe, he gains
the envious enmity of those who would destroy him.
During four years of sustained effort he drives everyone,
especially himself. What most people take for arrogance
others see as brilliance. Then he is ready: Alone
in the concrete bunker checking one last time
those mechanisms that have taken destiny out of his hand
he paces in dawn's darkness waiting while the others sprawl
on desert sand in galactic deep silence until a light

even the blind can see mocking the sun followed by
sound that rattles his bones, seizing his soul:
He knows he has become death the destroyer of worlds.
In the full light of day, his grin is wider than a Cheshire cat's.
ACT THREE: Recognized the world over on the covers
of magazines, he works for world control of the power
he helped release, resists a bigger, better bomb,
then pays the bill that satisfies the bargain:
Coming under scrutiny, then sustained investigation,
he betrays his Marxist friend, loses his security clearance,
is exiled to direct an institute of scholars who have access
to the cosmos he is denied. Knocked for a mobius loop,
bitter from his loss, he declines interviews.
His flesh leaches from his bones.

# Bronowski in East Hampton

New Jersey—of all places.
   After such a voyage searching the cosmos
   from the smallest sphere to the most massive galaxy
   he finds himself here, the voyage rich but exhausting.
   Yet each place along the way teaches him something,
   reveals who he is, shapes him in its own way,
   shows him what it means to wear a human face.
   His origin Poland, his family of Jews flees to Germany
   then England. In both places he learns to read
   deciphering cryptic quiverings that resolve into words
   revealing great books: Goethe, Shakespeare, Newton, Einstein.
   Shapes, too, enthrall him; their study sends him
   to Cambridge where he follows the lead of his two
   great loves: mathematics that helps decode the structures
   of the world; literature that reveals the anguish and the glory
   of the human soul. He roams both realms with ease
   seeking identity through knowledge of the world
   and of the self.
   Both worlds grow dark with twisted minds, twisted crosses,
   a hideous raging plague of technical destruction forged
   to perfection. To save himself, he writes of William Blake
   by midnight lamp while daily plotting bomb paths for deadly
   raids that bloom to firestorms over Dresden and Hamburg.
   Then Hiroshima where the moonlit ruins he roams reflect
   the evil in his own face, the harsh hard results of what his
   most dear friends had conceived: From the womb of the mind
   the deadliest progeny can never be unborn. He flees these furies
   to western beaches where on the ledge of the continent he pursues
   redemption attempting to resolve the mystery of our condition,
   those specific traits of our species that make us who we are.

From there, the bone-wearying tour to places where
the long human ascent has blossomed.
Broadcast by the most recent marvelous invention, the program
makes him famous: cab drivers know him by name; people
on New York sidewalks stop him, proclaim joy at the message
he has brought. He begins his final journey here in the home
of friends: Lingering illness made worse by incessant lifelong work,
heavy humid August heat seizes his heart. Before his final day
has hardly begun he drops to darkness, plunging toward the pit
that will bear his fossil remains.

# Eiseley in the City of Brotherly Love

His life is advent.
　　As a child hardly uttering words
　　he is lifted on his father's shoulders
　　toward the heavens and the Great Comet
　　that will return only when he is old,
　　should he live that long, so his father
　　whispers in the dark against the vast
　　canopy of stars while they anticipate
　　its first coming. Then it is gone fanning
　　a trail of fire and ice leaving behind
　　a child haunted while throughout his years
　　that bright crystal ball hurls through empty night
　　in an endless ellipse
　　Chance tests him for fitness: Something
　　in his genes allows him to survive: He flees
　　the isolation of his deaf mother's embrace
　　that trembles on the edge of madness
　　threatening to suck him in. Fighting off disease
　　that would drown his lungs. He sets out riding
　　boxcars, escapes being thrown from a speeding train
　　by a brakeman who sees in his transience an accusation
　　that raises self-righteous rage, then waking from sleep
　　as he clings to the underbelly of a tanker just as he slips
　　toward rails that race beneath massive grinding wheels.
　　Seeking knowledge, he wanders graveyards of the past,
　　digging up bones, studying them as oracles, seeking signs
　　of the chance change affecting his destiny: perhaps
　　a massive boulder sent from the stars raising tidal waves
　　of spume blocking the sun, starving giant reptiles
　　allowing the rodent that survives become an insomniac

wandering city streets at night, indifferent to any earthly
dangers, haunted by images captured in light, carried in
neural firings of his brain from one life station to another:
Rats rustling over moldering books in abandoned cellars;
a wagon and driver crossing a busy intersection or caught
in a sudden glare of lightning against a knurled tree
exposing a face twisted by some curse or accidental
gene; a worker in a city landfill beside a stalled rail
coach forking up steaming remnants of a doll, recalling
stillborns swaddled in newsprint abandoned in garbage
dumps; the beach at sunrise on which he makes his stand
helping on impulse a stranger hurl stranded starfish
back to the sea beyond the breaking surf.
His brief years are a primer: Burdened with consciousness,
a singularity in the starry cosmos, puzzled by the vagaries
of the path he follows in a blind search for deity that always
hides its face in mystery, his flesh, his father's fatal legacy
betrays him, turns on him, devouring him while the great
sweep of comet rushes on through the vast void gliding
back finally toward the Sun, childless, beneath the steady
knife of a stranger's firm hand, he goes into the dark alone.

# Hawking in the Nebula on the Sword of Orion

He would never amount to beans, so goes
     the bet of boyhood friends. He is slow
     to read; he stumbles often. His schooling
     undistinguished, he works just hard enough
     to let his brilliance shine; he parties:
     Dressed in splendid formal wear, his full
     fleshy cheeks tight as a chipmunk's,
     debonair, he has it made: the world
     of the new science, elegant, ripe apple,
     will drop into his hand when he opens it.
     His clumsiness increases. Diagnosed
     as having a disease without cure,
     he takes to his room, listens to Wagner,
     reads science fiction, drinks heavily
     distracted by his Quarry from playing
     the game of universe: Grand Unification
     that weds relativity to quantum physics.
     He becomes prisoner of his own body:
     with no control, he cannot dress or feed
     himself, relies on others around the clock
     for care. A woman's love helps. His own
     courage and humor intact, he becomes
     a paradigm of energy struggling on
     crutches to bed then confined to a motorized
     chair squeezing out six words a minute on a monitor,
     ending later with a voice simulator through
     which he speaks in a synthetic voice.
     Yet, his intellect is free to roam.

Armed with mathematics and intuition
he stalks The Quarry trying to read
its mind: His search without observation
more faith than knowledge gives rise
to miracles: black hole singularities
with event horizons that bang inward
like trapdoors sealing off the universe
from the spider within: virtual particles
with strange contingent existences,
random fluctuations, their position
and momentum never truly known.
Then the boldest move of all: cancel
Singularity: the cosmos has no edge,
no boundary, was not created, will
never be destroyed. It simply Is.
What place, then, for a Creator?
He offers his regret with a slack-jawed grin.
So he moves on. His thoughts coming
from some vast distance reaching us
a question at a time, he wears a halo:
Cloaked in a spiritual aura as his substance
sloughs toward nothingness, his mind expands
nova-like toward the infinite: His friends declare:
"He's going to end up a saint."

# Secular Saints—Second Series
## Arnold at Liverpool

Son of a famous preacher he issues into the world
    the year Beethoven passes into the dark, the year
    Napoleon grows smaller but large in stature laid
    in the monumental tomb that expands into a shrine,
    the little corporal still commanding the adulation
    of those lingering languishing alive diminished
    by the fleeting glory of so many lost in the bitter
    cold sweeping vast terrain of Russia.
    While the preacher's son still young gathers fame
    in his own right through poetry that retains the taint
    of Romance lingering from Wordsworth, a friend
    and mentor, his brooding verse snags the dilemma
    of Victorian, post-Darwinian culture: "wandering
    between two worlds one dead the other powerless
    to be born."
    In his later years, he grows large—twelve stone,
    some surmise—from too much social feasting,
    too frequent the seemingly endless travels
    inspecting schools, too many hours setting down
    his immediate observations, more hours still
    setting out his insights on culture, literature,
    religion, the poetic spirit of his early life
    and work dissipating with his increasing
    girth and rise in social standing.
    How many such conflicts has he witnessed
    as aide or clerk (so lowly a title?) son of
    that famous preacher father who dies suddenly
    of a weak then failed heart still young in mind.

Now the son—sometimes surprised at surviving
this long yet mindful of his heritage—succumbs
to the same fatal flaw at the end of the century,
near the end of an era, the weight he has gained
with reputation now shocking him in his leap
over the low border fence trying a playful
attempt to redeem his youthful energy and spirit
while waiting for the return of his married daughter
from the States. Seeking rejuvenation he instead
stumbles into the dark.

# Sartre in Saint Germain des Pres

Born into the bourgeoisie, raised in comfort,
    well dressed, he attends middleclass schools
    then with his diploma teaches but joins others
    to meet the invading Nazi horde.
    Captured in the rout at the Maginot Line designed
    to keep out barbarians, he spends his captivity
    reading philosophy, ironically German:
    Husserl, Heidegger, Nietzsche while setting out
    his own voluminous response to the enigma
    regarding existence in being and nothingness.
    Finally released, he joins the Resistance, starts
    a review of current political, epistemological,
    perceptual theories while writing plays
    celebrating the Absurd, one that depicts Hell as other
    people.
    After liberation from German tyranny, he returns
    to teaching in Cherbourg where he sets out his ideas
    in an innovative method through fiction. But the seaside
    dreariness and mud force him to flee his existential reality,
    settling at last in Paris—where else—The Left Bank, the Sorbonne,
    an *appartement* just off the plaza named for the grand structure
    of faith that dominates and labels the *arrondissement*:
    Outside the tall, eighteenth century windows of his flat above
    the cellar brasserie and plaza before the ancient abbey that harbors
    Descartes' tomb, a pointed pile of soaring stone, relic of faith
    that names the dead-end paved boulevard running up toward
    Montmartre beside other eighteenth century apartments
    with coved ceilings and floral trim, past gouged cornerstones
    with bullet holes from repeated wars, he perceives the milieu
    of pedestrians and endless traffic, cafés with neon signs

that glow midday, and, of course, Les Deux Maggots where
he goes as diligently as ritual for *café noir* and *croissants*, nestled
behind piles of books he reads and reviews in blue swirling smoke
of cigarettes or pipe. Here, too, or next door at le Café' du Flore,
for years he gathers with others in a movement he defines listening
to Merleau-Ponty discourse on phenomenological perception,
jousting with Camus on the truth of dialectical materialism.
Picasso drops in from time to time to scratch his balding head
at such perplexing discussions.
Most days when she's not working on her own ideas regarding
Feminism, Simone Beauvoir graces his table until he moves with her
out into the soft rain, climbs with her the stairway to their rooms
where they settle at their desks, he fueling his ideas with Speed
washed down with whiskey building a mountain of paper to produce
a mouse working until evening when they descend again to the plaza
and a nearby restaurant, perhaps the cave of the brasserie below.
So his numbered days continue: He writes more plays, sets out
the tenants of existentialism, investigates through words situations
that define the primary choice determining the direction and the moments
of peoples' lives: Tintoretto, Genet. He becomes estranged from Camus
over Soviet imperialism under the guise of Marxism. Later, he sits
as both prosecutor and chief justice at a trial he conducts indicting
the United States government for its actions in Southeast Asia.
He is offered the Nobel for his work that he declines as ostentation
yet is awarded the prize anyway. Always busy then finally weary
and aging and ill from his constant efforts, he seeks redemption
under the warm Italian sun but returns to Paris where at last

his being slips into nothingness.

# Envoi

Each in his own way
    these mortals searched
    for Spirit, found the pilgrimage
    a struggle up the steep and treacherous
    mountain path where demons and angels—
    both messengers—challenged
    them to wrestle their way past.
    They did not cling easily to faith,
    hobbling on it like a crutch.
    They faced the void without support,
    their doubt their strength, their curiosity
    the key to wonder, opening them to the mystery
    and the glory of the world.

# Acknowledgments

Some poems in this collection appeared in the following publications:

The Clearing: "Barn Cleaning," "The Sacrament," "Fourth Floor North," "The Whale," "Sanctuary," "Nonce on a Theme by Williams," "A Poem for All Occasions," "Civilization and Its Dissonance," "Reconnaissance," "A Poem for Sancho," "Mexican Bus Ride"

Covington Library: "Leaving the Yellow House"

Espial: "The Bounty"

The Green River Review: "Dependency," "Northwest Passage," "Leave Taking," "A Poem for Sancho," "Camus in Sens"

The Guild: "The Sewerage Problem at Versailles," "Arboretum," "Fortunate Flaw." "Song," "Poem," "Contemplation"

Mind Lyric: "Theme and Variation, ""Poem, "Forced March"

Mirror Northwest: "The Haunting," "Mea Culpa"

Spring Lyric: "The Vision," " 'The Prairie," "Epithalamium," "Through a Glass Darkly," "A Communion of Saints," "Windfall"

Spring Rain: "The Prelude," "Kiji Thinking," "Accident/Incident"

# Afterword

Most poems I offer in this collection were written over several decades during which I resided in the Pacific Northwest and some, those in the section 47 Degrees North, obviously indicate my response to Northwest environment. However, others, those especially in the section The Portable Cage are a progressive poetic response to some events in my own development that I have narrated in *A Stirring of the Air, A Shifting of the Light*. Still others offer my perspective of various places to which I traveled, and the poems in Secular Saints, the last section, indicate my response to the lives of people who have had a significant influence on the history of ideas, a subject that I have followed with great interest throughout most of my life.

A few words regarding my poetic style might be appropriate and useful: I rarely use rhyme and employ it only when using a traditional poetic form such as the villanelle. Instead, I use what William Carlos Williams referred to as the variable foot. The use of such a foot leads to varying line lengths and spacing by means of which the breaking of lines conveys or emphasizes the poetic image and meaning by words that end the lines. This technique too often has been affected by the restrictive limits and frequent challenges imposed my MSWord and the template format of Kindle Direct Publishing and Smashword for publishing in ebook from. I also use rhythm to emphasize imagery, and I use wording enhanced through alliteration, internal rhyme, assonance, and consonance to highlight imagery. The result of these poetic techniques should suggest how the poem should read as if it were read aloud, thus carrying the original sense of "poem" having its origin in music and song.

Poetic influences other than Williams might be implied by my use of allusion or direct purloining of lines and methods from other poets: William Wordsworth, Matthew Arnold, William Butler Yeats, Dylan Thomas, Wallace Stevens, Theodore Roethke, Allen Ginsberg, and, of course, Walt Whitman—and most likely others whom I have absorbed unwittingly through poetic osmosis.

However, despite such perhaps somewhat obvious poetic influences, I am confident that I have offered my own unique poetic response to the events I have encountered during my decades of journeying around the Sun. Yet, as to the justness of my claim I leave to you who might honor my sauntering by having taken up this book. For as old Walt said in "Song of Myself," "Who touches this book touches a man."

# Don't miss out!

Visit the website below and you can sign up to receive emails whenever Wayne Luckmann publishes a new book. There's no charge and no obligation.

https://books2read.com/r/B-A-AJAW-HGJUC

**BOOKS2READ**

Connecting independent readers to independent writers.

# Also by Wayne Luckmann

**Rate of Exchange**
Sleeping through the Revolution
Sweet Journey Home
All Things Can Tempt Me From My Craft of Verse
Go and Catch a Falling Star
A Free and Open Nature
Rate of Exchange

**Standalone**
The Inhabited Garden
A Stirring of the Air, A Shifting of the Light
The Buried Life
Northwest Passage